821
J81B
C392b

A C

A CELEBRATION OF BEN JONSON

PAPERS PRESENTED AT
THE UNIVERSITY OF TORONTO IN OCTOBER 1972
EDITED BY
WILLIAM BLISSETT JULIAN PATRICK R.W. VAN FOSSEN

UNIVERSITY OF TORONTO PRESS

TORONTO AND BUFFALO

©
University
of
Toronto
Press
1973
Toronto and Buffalo
Reprinted in paperback 1975
Printed in USA
ISBN 0-8020-2133-9 (cloth)
ISBN 0-8020-6284-9 (paper)
LC 73-91241

CONTENTS

vi

CONTRIBUTORS

JONAS BARISH

Professor of English, University of California. Author of
Ben Jonson and the Language of Prose Comedy
(Harvard 1960)

GEORGE HIBBARD

Professor of English, University of Waterloo. Author of
Thomas Nashe (Routledge & Kegan Paul 1962)

L.C. KNIGHTS

King Edward VII Professor of English Literature, Cambridge University. Author of *Drama and Society in the
Age of Jonson* (Chatto & Windus 1937)

CLIFFORD LEECH

Professor of English, University College, University of
Toronto. Author of many studies in Shakespeare and the
Elizabethan drama

D.F. MCKENZIE
Professor of English, Victoria University of Wellington.
Author of many bibliographical studies

HUGH MACLEAN
Professor of English, State University of New York at
Albany. Author of many essays on the poetry of the
English Renaissance

INTRODUCTION

Ben Jonson was born either in 1572 or in 1573, and it occurred to the rather large complement of Jonsonians in the various colleges of the University of Toronto that we might appropriately hold a conference in one of the anniversary years and publish the proceedings in the other. A committee was formed and drew up a programme of six papers. Happily, all six of the scholars we approached agreed to give papers; unhappily, a month before the conference was to be held Professor E.A. Armstrong of the University of London suffered an accident and had to withdraw, and so we have no special consideration of Ben Jonson as a man of the theatre and maker of masques. At short notice, Professor George Hibbard, who had already contributed greatly to the Jonson year as chairman of a conference at the University of Waterloo in July, stepped in with a fresh and well-considered paper. Each speaker came from a different institution, and Canada, the United States, Great Britain, and New Zealand were represented: we hope that the

balance of the papers likewise reflects the range of Ben
Jonson's achievement and the combination of brio and
control so characteristic of him.

It will be noticed that the papers arrange themselves
in pairs: the 'incredibility' of Jonson's comedy, as discussed by Professor Leech, is of a piece with the distrust
and defiance of the audience as discussed by Professor
Barish; Professors Hibbard and McKenzie offer critical
assessment of plays, the one wide-ranging, the other
closely focused on a previously neglected play; and
Professors Maclean and Knights, in different but complementary styles, approach the difficult and rewarding
task of defining Jonson's poetry of appraisal.

Since a book of this size and contents was planned
from the inception of the conference, it was impossible
for us to include in it the volunteered papers, successful
though they proved to be. Conferees will wish to be reminded and readers to be informed of these so that they
may be read when published in various journals. Professor Trevor Howard-Hill, of the Universities of Swansea
and South Carolina, outlined to the entire membership
his plan of a Ben Jonson concordance and later discussed
the complications of the project with a number of spe-
cialists at the point in our proceedings when we divided
into smaller groups. In one of these groups Professor
A.M. Leggatt, of University College in the University
of Toronto, read a paper on 'Morose and his Tormentors'
and Professor James Tulip, of the University of Sydney
in Australia, one on 'Jonson and the Political Life of his
Time.' In another, Professor Michael Tait, of Scarborough
College in the University of Toronto, spoke on 'The
Fool as Hero: An Apology for Epicure,' and Professor
Judith Gardiner, of the University of Illinois at Chicago
Circle, led a discussion of 'The Relationship of Jonson's
Poetry and Plays: Salient Issues.' The fourth group,
chaired by Professor John Meagher, of St Michael's

College in the University of Toronto, was concerned with university productions of Ben Jonson. Miss Mary Giffin and members of the acting, dancing, musical, and production staff of the Poculi Ludique Societas took part in a discussion of the PLS production of *Pleasure Reconcil'd to Virtue*, then playing. It is a pleasant duty to thank them for adding an extra performance so that all members of the conference had an opportunity to see this Jonson masque. Thanks also are due to Mrs Cynthia Heidenreich for the imaginative display of Inigo Jones designs for masques and masquers concurrently to be seen in the University Library.

Ben Jonson was a convivial man himself and excelled in devising entertainments for others. At a banquet held in Massey College, a toast to 'Rare Ben Jonson' was proposed by Professor Northrop Frye. Like the papers at the sessions, the toast combined lightness and seriousness, substance and rapidity, in Jonsonian measure. The banquet was followed by an Entertainment devised by Professor Robertson Davies, the Master of Massey, in the warmly inviting and festive Seeley Hall, Trinity College. The best way to thank Professor Davies and his troupe, or tribe, is to reproduce the programme of their ingenious, easy, and elegant 'Evening with Ben Jonson.'

It is a pleasure to thank the chairmen of the plenary sessions, Professor R.A. Greene, Dean of Arts and Science; Professor Ann Saddlemyer, Director of the Graduate Centre for the Study of Drama; and Professor Gerald Eades Bentley, of Princeton University. As chairman of the organizing committee I must also list and thank its members. It comprised Clifford Leech (who was drafted to give a paper within minutes of our constituting ourselves), Brian Parker and Millar MacLure (who missed the conference because of leave-of-absence but were most helpful at the inception), F.D. Hoeniger, Hugh MacCallum, J.M.R. Margeson, John Meagher, Allan

On Friday, October 27
in Seeley Hall, Trinity College
an Entertainment
is offered to The Ben Jonson Conference, entitled

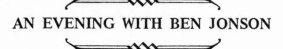

AN EVENING WITH BEN JONSON

comprised of selections from the lyrical, satirical and dramatic Works, cullings from *Jonsonus Virbius,* the Conversations with Drummond of Hawthornden, and comment by critics whose words will be so immediately familiar to the learned audience that it were nugatory to identify them.

READERS

Primus	*Martin Hunter*
Secundus	*Judy Hunter*
Tertius	*Rex Southgate*
Quartus	*Molly Thom*
Quintus	*Eric Binnie*
Sextus	*Brenda Davies*

The Massey College Singers, under the direction of Gordon Wry, Esq., will sing *Slow, slow fresh fount,* by Henry Youll — of whom little is known, but who was the composer of the music for *Cynthia's Revels,* and who set this Jonson lyric in his *Canzonets for 3 Voices (1605); A Hymn to Diana,* composed by John Cook for the Stratford Festival (1955); and *Charis, Her Triumph,* composed by Ralph Vaughan Williams (1929).

The distinguished audience is entreated
not to restrain its expressions of delight

The entertainment devised and directed by Robertson Davies

Pritchard, and R.W. Van Fossen, who took charge of arranging the volunteered papers at the Saturday morning session. A.M. Leggatt served as Secretary in 1970–1 and returned from leave in time to give further invaluable aid during the conference. Julian Patrick was secretary in 1971–2: he proved indispensable in matters of policy as well as in all the innumerable practicalities. He and Professor Van Fossen have done so much additional work toward the preparation of this volume that the least I could do was to insist that their names appear as co-editors.

The then Acting President of the University, Dr J.H. Sword, from the first took a generous personal interest in the celebration of Ben Jonson. The conference was made possible by grants from the University and the Canada Council, and the publication of the book by grants from the University of Toronto and the Humanities Research Council of Canada, using funds provided by the Canada Council. To Dr Sword and to these institutions we offer our thanks – and to the University of Toronto Press for the confidence shown in the project from its inception.

Finally we must thank the conferees for coming from far and near, for their alert attention and lively trade of ideas, and for giving every appearance of enjoying themselves in Ben Jonson's company.

WFB
UNIVERSITY COLLEGE
UNIVERSITY OF TORONTO

A CELEBRATION OF
BEN JONSON

THE INCREDIBILITY OF JONSONIAN COMEDY

CLIFFORD LEECH

All comedy is a matter of make-believe. I need not talk much about the Greeks – either about Aristophanes, who gave us splendid cartoons of the anti-establishment, and occasionally of the establishment, figures that he wanted to rebuke, or about Menander, who gave us, as his successors Plautus and Terence did, the idea of absurdity that he and they saw prevailing in family life. All of these dramatists knew that things as they are were indeed incredible, and urged on us their exaggerations as a way of making us recognise that our own lives could not possibly be envisaged if we did not know they truly exist.

Let us, then, first direct our attention to the English drama that preceded Jonson. In the miracle plays we have the comedy-in-counterpoint that so splendidly characterises the Wakefield *Secunda Pastorum*, the sheer fun that is present in all the plays about Noah, the 'dark' comedy that finds its place in the York *Crucifixion*, where the nailing of Christ to the Cross is made a matter of laughter to the torturers, though not, surely, to the spec-

3

tators. We shall need to remember this when we come to
Ben Jonson. But comedy for the early Elizabethans was
either a momentary relief or an echoing of Latin comedy
or a wandering tale of adventure and love such as Sidney
castigated in *An Apology for Poetry*. We have few plays
surviving in this last kind from the 1570s and 1580s, but
Common Conditions and *Sir Clyamon and Clamydes*,
the latter providing us with the earliest surviving example of a girl disguised as a boy, give us some idea of
the sort of play that Sidney did not think much of.[1] If
we turn to Shakespeare's earliest comedies, we must
have in mind *The Comedy of Errors* (an obvious deriva-
tive from Plautus, but going beyond him in its doubling
of the twins), *Love's Labour's Lost* (a highly sophistical
version of what Lyly had done), and *The Two Gentlemen
of Verona*, perhaps his earliest comedy, certainly a
'wandering' play indeed, linking the already established
love-friendship theme with the boy-girl disguise, the
'romantic' setting, and a new note of subdued mockery
that was beginning to come in. Greene had done, in *Friar
Bacon and Friar Bungay* and *James* iv, a similar sort of
thing, while eschewing the mockery. Peele made more
obvious fun of love and friendship in *The Old Wives'
Tale*.[2] We can say that from the early 1590s to around
1600 we have an alternation between romance, never
quite believed in by Shakespeare at this time (not even
in *As You Like It* and *Twelfth Night*), and the Plautine
comedy of intrigue, notably illustrated in Henry Porter's
The Two Angry Women of Abingdon. No one indeed
could believe deeply in any of it: these were plays to
tickle the fancy, only at moments reminding us of the
way things are. Jonson did similar things in his earliest
plays, *The Case is Altered* and *Every Man in His Humour*,
but a difference began to manifest itself soon.

Every Man in His Humour was, we are told, recommended by Shakespeare to the Lord Chamberlain's com-

4

pany. Perhaps he saw that here was a kind of co
that belonged far more truly to the Plautine manner than
his own *Comedy of Errors* had done: here was no 'serious framework,' no ultimate and pious resolution; Jonson
was indeed not pious here, except in relation to the
ancients, and was to grow increasingly sharp-tongued in
the plays of the ensuing years. Moreover, his use of the
'humours,' both 'true' and 'false,' gave to the play an
intellectual muscularity that made it reach adventurously
beyond Plautus. Shakespeare himself was never, I think,
to give more than a cursory nod in the direction of the
'humours,' although Professor J.W. Draper has urged on
us the idea that he leaned much on them.[3] If the legend
that Shakespeare recommended the play has a basis in
fact, his tribute to Jonson on this occasion is as important
as Jonson's to him in the First Folio verses and in *Discoveries*. At this point we should perhaps remind ourselves
that in the Induction to *Every Man Out of His Humour*
Jonson was to talk of 'humours' in relation to the drama
as primarily valid in a metaphoric sense: he was no longer
to be tied to the exemplification of the traditional four;
he was to work with vividly imagined though strictly de-
limited *dramatis personae* who have little more to do
with the traditional humours than have the figures of
Aristophanes. But in his first two plays for Shakespeare's
company he had labelled himself the 'humours' dramatist, and the label stuck. He lived with it, and called what
was probably his last completed play *The Magnetic Lady,
or Humours Reconciled*. The result has been that the
general criticism of his work has laboured to see his
figures as more diagrammatic than in truth they are.

So with that glance of recognition at the 'humours,'
let us try to forget them. What matters much more is
that his plays customarily defy our ability to believe in
what they present to us. We may look back for a moment
at *Every Man Out of His Humour*, the truly seminal play

5

COMEDY

.imself free from the strait-
.ecessor by the Lord Chamber-
a disaster on the stage but was
.at followed. It contains the scene
. Puntarvolo every day greets his wife
. seen her before and falls in love with
. is is manifestly absurd and incredible, yet
.nd of sense: to see one's wife as a person
eve... .s to give a true meaning to marriage, even
though .e ordinary mortals cannot usually manage it.
Of course, the ultimately right attitude is to recognise
the known while still being astonished by the unknown,
yet Puntarvolo has at least got half-way there. The fact
that the observers in the play mock at him is a reflection
much more on their limitations than on his. The incredible has here become at least partially the necessary.
Throughout, indeed, Jonson employs exaggeration to
make a valid point: when Sordido anguishes over the
probable loss of the imagined grain in his stores, he is
merely presenting in an extreme way what the *entrepre-
neur* – or 'developer,' shall we say – customarily spends
his mind on.

Wherever Jonson set his scene, his thought was principally of the London of his time. In the revision of *Every
Man in His Humour* he shifted the scene from Italy to
England; he wrote *The Poetaster* with a setting in the
Rome of Augustus, but referred in it to theatres on the
other side of the Tiber, clearly indicating the Bankside;
he felt urged to introduce Sir Politick and Lady Would-
be and Peregrine into the Venice of *Volpone*. So Fletcher,
learning much from him, was later to set *The Maid's
Tragedy* and *The Humorous Lieutenant* in remote places
but was to present us with pictures of court-scenes that
belonged clearly to Whitehall. His master Ben Jonson
always balanced the remote with the near, the incredible
along with the recognisable. Yet incredible in some

measure it always was. His London in *The Alchemist* was enduring the plague – by no means incredible, of course, in those days, yet incredible in relation to the intrigues of that particular play. Here, after all, is great fun in a time of plague. *Bartholomew Fair* was also rooted to London, yet what could be more outrageous than the things that we know, as he knew, to have existed there – the affair of Ursula the pig-woman's other leg; the peripatetic Trouble-all, the madman; the overweening yet pathetic belief of Mr Justice Overdo that he can control 'enormities'? Overdo in his disguise could be, I dare to say, an echo of Shakespeare's Duke Vincentio in *Measure for Measure* – so sure of himself, so forced ultimately into acquiescence with the ways of the world. Vincentio set off into a pretended exile, affirming that he wanted the law to be more strictly enforced than he had personally dared to make it; yet at the end he distributed pardons to everyone (except the Lucio who had mocked at him), even to the manifestly and deeply guilty Barnardine, and wanted to marry the novice Isabella. There was a splendid production of this play at Stratford-upon-Avon in 1970, in which Isabella turned away from the Duke at the end and he had to make the best of it: that was, I think, a fully justified reading of the text, although Shakespeare has given us only Isabella's silence to go upon. Overdo similarly spies, similarly has to abdicate. His name may echo that of Mistress Overdone in Shakespeare's play. He cannot keep things up when he sees that his wife has fallen in with the most outrageous elements in the Fair. All he can do is to invite everyone home to supper, which in effect is what Vincentio did in Shakespeare's play. The relation between Jonson and Shakespeare here has, I think, been commonly overlooked. Both of them invite our disbelief, and defy it.

Jonson, like all of his contemporaries in the early seventeenth century, loved to play tricks. In *Volpone* he presents us with many incredibilities. First, how could Volpone get away with it for so long? He rises in the morning to worship his 'saint' when the 'shrine' has been revealed: this is a parody of a Christian man's morning worship at his private oratory. We must, I think, imagine a prie-dieu available for him to kneel at. The long opening speech is full of scriptural references. Yet, immediately after his devotions have been done, he claims that – in accepted moral terms – his way is far less blameworthy than that of the world he knows outside:

> *Yet, I glory*
> *More in the cunning purchase of my wealth,*
> *Then in the glad possession; since I gaine*
> *No common way: I vse no trade, no venter;*
> *I wound no earth with plow-shares; fat no beasts*
> *To feede the shambles; have no mills for yron,*
> *Oyle, corne, or men, to grinde 'hem into poulder;*
> *I blow no subtill glasse; expose no ships*
> *To threatnings of the furrow-faced sea;*
> *I turne no moneys, in the publike banke;*
> *Nor vsure priuate –* [1.i.30–40][4]

It will be noted that the people Volpone feels he is superior to include both Shylock and Antonio. Immediately afterwards we get the 'show' presented by Nano, Androgyno, and Castrone concerning the present embodiment of the soul of Pythagoras: it descends from the philosopher to the fool, who is both man and woman, who is indeed Everyman, a parody in advance of Eliot's Tiresias in *The Waste Land*. In the song that follows their show, the fool is exalted: '*O, who would not be / Hee, hee, hee?*' (1.ii.80–1) The suggestion of laughter in the double sense of '*Hee, hee, hee*' is Jonson's ironic comment on what can happen to the philosopher.

~~Then~~ Volpone gets Mosca to persuade his would-be heirs to insult him, as they are made to believe that he is beyond hearing in his sickness. Moreover, it is obvious that the character-names are mocking: almost every character is reduced to animal or insect – fox, gadfly, vulture, crow, raven, kite and, for Peregrine, falcon. The use of type-names was long established from the moral plays of the fifteenth and sixteenth centuries, but this lowering to the beast-world was new. But the Fox himself trades on the others' special peculiarities as animal-figures. He gets Corvino to bring his wife to him, Corbaccio to disinherit his heir, Voltore to do his work in the court. He even gets Celia to throw her handkerchief to him when he poses as the mountebank Scoto of Mantua: this is perhaps his most brilliant trick, the thing that truly surpasses. When he fails in his attempt to seduce or rape her, it seems only because Jonson has dallied with a double trick, having Mosca bring in Bonario to watch his father's disinheriting of him yet inadvertently in time to rescue Celia from rape. The coincidence troubles us, but it keeps the play within the bounds of comedy – at least for the moment – and at the same time is part of what Jonson wants here, the further challenge to our credulity. Again, when Volpone and Mosca do so splendidly in their first appearance in the court, we are brought up against the question, How can they do it? But they *act* so well that the court is powerless: only the innocent Celia and Bonario speak the truth, and that is not enough. Perhaps Webster remembered this when he had his Vittoria successfully defy the court to find her guilty of murder. Then Volpone wants to stretch everyone's credulity further: he will pretend to be dead, with Mosca his heir, thus defeating every would-be heir, he thinks. But that defeats only himself, and he cannot accept defeat by Mosca. Rather than that, he will betray himself at whatever cost. And he is splendid when he hears his dreadful sentence: 'This is call'd mortifying of a FOXE' (v.xii.125). The sentences of the prime malefactors are,

stop

of course, breath-taking. Voltore, Corvino, Corbaccio are made to endure a mere humiliation, like Sir Politick too, but Volpone and Mosca have living deaths in front of them. And this is a court manifestly corrupt as well as stupid, where one of the judges has so recently aspired to making the new magnifico Mosca his son-in-law. We are again defied to believe; but we must believe, for this is the way things are.

It is evident where Jonson's sympathy ultimately lies. Volpone speaks the epilogue, as Face a few years later did in *The Alchemist*. In the English Renaissance plays the speaker of the epilogue is normally – not always (we may think of the King of France in *All's Well that Ends Well*) – the character who has not only made the strongest impact on the audience but is the one closest to the author's heart. The epilogue is in some measure an apologia. Here Volpone says that, though he is punished by the laws, there is 'no suffring due / For any fact, which he hath done 'gainst you.' There could hardly be a clearer instance of a dramatist at least partially exculpating his character by means of a theatrical device. Yet Jonson in the Dedication of *Volpone* to the two universities urged that his play had an appropriate moral ending. I shall comment further on this later. For the moment I can merely remark that this is not how the comedy works in the theatre. In the end we are on Volpone's side, though of course it is deplorable, and incredible, that we should be.

Some years before this Jonson had written for the boy-players, in *Cynthia's Revels* and *The Poetaster*, and was to do so later in *Epicene*. There he was indeed brought up against the almost impossible gap between the passions presented and the conceivable way of presenting them. Later Shakespeare was to make his boy-player in the part of Cleopatra imagine how, in the Rome she would have been taken to if she had not killed herself, a squeaking Cleopatra might have boyed her greatness. So Marston in *Antonio's Revenge*, I.v, makes the old Pandulpho, played of course by a boy, ask how he can properly act out his grief for his son's loss:

> *Would'st have me cry, run raving up & down,*
> *For my sons losse? would'st have me turn rank mad,*
> *Or wring my face with mimic action;*
> *Stampe, curse, weepe, rage & then my bosom strike?*
> *Away tis apish action, player-like.*[5]

There is a double irony here. The boy cannot truly play the character's part, yet he mocks at any sort of 'player-like' action. So in II.iii of this play the boy playing Antonio is made to reject the 'affected straines' of the 'Tragedian':

> *Madam, I will not swell like a Tragedian, in forced passion of affected straines ...*

and in IV.v Pandulpho makes a specific reference to the child-actors:

> *Why, all this while I ha but plaid a part,*
> *Like to some boy, that actes a Tragedie,*
> *Speakes burly words, and raves out passion:*
> *But, when he thinks upon his infant weaknesse,*
> *He droopes his eye.*

Harvey Wood in his edition of Marston suggests that this may make us think that the play came to be acted by adults before its publication in 1602.[6] We might as well think that Shakespeare envisaged his Cleopatra being acted by a woman. Jonson gives us the ultimate irony on this matter in his witty and moving epitaph on Salomon Pavy, the boy who at the age of thirteen was adept at playing old men's parts for the children's performances, and was, Jonson suggests, killed by the Fates because they thought he was truly old and therefore ripe for death. Here a major writer for the children pays his tribute to the expertise of an outstanding boy, and yet recognizes that it seemed to go beyond belief.

Even so, Jonson claimed to be the 'realist' of his time. Everyone knows the Prologue to *Every Man in His Humour* which was first included in the 1616 Folio edition of the play. He mocks at the playwrights who

> make a child, now swadled, to proceede
> Man, and then shoote vp, in one beard, and weede,
> Past threescore yeeres ... [Prologue, 11. 7–9]

who

> with three rustie swords,
> And helpe of some few foot-and-halfe-foote words,
> Fight ouer Yorke, and Lancasters long iarres ...
> [11. 9–11]

who with '*Chorus* wafts you ore the seas' (1. 14), who bring a 'creaking throne' down, and let off a 'nimble squibbe ... to make afear'd / The gentlewomen' (11. 16–18). Shakespeare and Marlowe and the playwrights that Sidney mocked in the *Apology* all seem under attack here. Jonson's own way, he says, will be different: when comedy is to show 'an Image of the times, / And sport with humane follies, not with crimes ...,' she will present 'deedes, and language, such as men doe vse ...' (11. 21–4). Of course, Jonson did not always merely 'sport with humane follies, not with crimes': much as we are, ultimately, on Volpone's side, we can hardly say that he or, for that matter, Mosca and Voltore and Corbaccio and Corvino are free from crime. Nor can we say that of Face, Subtle, Doll, Lovewit, or indeed of some of their gulls. And if he goes beyond mere folly, he also goes beyond the belief that we normally like to extend to the imaginable ways of men. Recently, for the 1972 Stratford-upon-Avon Shakespeare Conference, I wrote a paper on 'The Incredible in

Jacobean Tragedy,' where I argued that the defiance of what we should like to believe in the world around us – which is surely characteristic of those contemporaries of Jonson who wrote primarily in the tragic Kind – is, in fact, true to our deepest understanding of that world. Because Jonson was a major dramatist, he too had to include in his major plays a frank recognition of the nature of evil. That is why the court in *Volpone* is corrupt, why the punishments of Volpone and Mosca are extreme. It is not that all courts are corrupt, all punishments vicious; but the major dramatist has to present the worst as well as the best, and in the world around us the worst makes perhaps the stronger bid for our attention. Besides, we want to close our eyes to it, and one of the tasks of the writer – particularly the most public kind of writer, the dramatist – is to keep those eyes open. So, when he is at his greatest stretch, he offers us not 'sport' but the things we might forget.

This is a different thing from the mere trading on popular resentment against authority, such as we can find in the lesser drama of England and the United States today. Jonson aimed at inducing the true shock of recognition in his major plays, not merely complacent 'hurrahs' from the already happily dissident.

Yet in their later years Shakespeare and Jonson in their different ways pushed ever onwards into the yet more incredible. In *Bartholomew Fair* Jonson could do this while still keeping to the London scene, presenting the 'possible' though still breath-taking. He could introduce the mad Trouble-all and the more than usually incompetent Justice; he could put the Justice into the stocks – as infamous a thing as Cornwall's putting there the King's messenger in *King Lear*, yet here presented with a purely ludicrous effect; he could make the Justice's law-giving at the end turn into an invitation to supper; he could make Winwife and Quarlous choose the names 'Argalus' (from the *Arcadia*) and 'Palamon' (probably from *The Two Noble Kinsmen*), giving to these on-the-make young men a curious connection with two romantic writings, one of high authority, one a somewhat acid thing written a year earlier than Jonson's play. That we may see *The Two Noble Kinsmen* as 'acid' does not mean that Jonson would see it so: he is more likely to have felt it belonged with Shakespeare's other final romances, which he attacked more than once. *Bartholomew Fair* is indeed shot through with ineffective justice, madness, 'romance' taken up cynically, and the general and triumphant wantonness of the Fair.

From that he probably went on to *The Devil is an Ass*, where the general idea is that of Hilaire Belloc's epigram:

> *The devil, having nothing else to do,*
> *Set out to tempt my Lady Poltagrue;*
> *My Lady, tempted by a private whim,*
> *To his intense annoyance, tempted him.*

In this play there is a return to the manner of the six-teenth-century moral plays, but with Jonson's character-istic difference. The devil, as in Belloc, is given a low status indeed: who needs him now, we are asked? So the old thing is turned on its head, and we are challenged to say that we need the old theology when we in ourselves are so corrupt. This by no means implies that Jonson himself would want the old theology away: he mocks at our apparent freedom from the need. This is one of his outstanding minor plays, like the undeservedly abused *A Tale of a Tub*, probably written (at least in its first form) much earlier but providing a remarkable exposition of the craziness of the simple life, similar to what is given to us through the true inhabitants, as distinct from the visitors, in *Bartholomew Fair*.

Shakespeare, abandoning first the merely legendary or fictional story that had availed him in *Hamlet, Othello,*

14

Lear, and *Macbeth*, went on to use Plutarch for a time, needing once more a root in history after his almost complete, and anguishing, independence of 'fact' in the previous tragedies. Then came *Pericles* and the subsequent romances, from old tales or pure imagining. 'Let the impossible come' seemed to be his cue for making further exploration. When, after *Pericles*, he had got started on this way, he may well have been struck by what Beaumont and Fletcher were already doing, although *Pericles* surely came before *Philaster* and we cannot regard his younger contemporaries as giving him the initiative for his final plays.[7] Yet increasingly he came to defy 'credibility' – not, as he had done earlier, because he was following a dramatic fashion, but because incredibility had come to be what he lived with. His theophanies – of Diana in *Pericles*, of Jupiter in *Cymbeline*, of the unseen Apollo in *The Winter's Tale*, of the only indirectly manifested Diana and Venus and Mars in *The Two Noble Kinsmen* (and there is not much doubt that Shakespeare was responsible for the scene in which these gods make their existence felt) – are not what he would have urged on us earlier. His ghosts and witches in the tragedies do not matter to this degree, for they can be interpreted as dramatic conveniences, as token reminders of the other world and of the principle of evil that exists within us. His theophanies in the final plays enter inexorably.

Jonson does not go so far as this. He has no theophanies in his final plays: he reserved such things for the masque. For the most part he returned to the satires and the 'humours.' We have already seen that *The Magnetic Lady* had the alternative title *Humours Reconciled*, and in *The Staple of News* he splendidly represented the craze for money and the craze for news, in an age mercifully dependent on rumour, not newspapers. But in *The New Inn, or The Light Heart* he gave us something near to Shakespeare's last plays, yet without a god's blessing or rebuke, without even – as in *The Tempest* – a demi-god's overriding authority. Yet the disguised Lord Frampul, the host of the New Inn, echoes in some measure the Prospero of some eighteen years before. It is characteristic of Jonson that this man is only the host of an inn, though a lord too, not the magician who controls the island he has taken over. Prospero had been obliged to leave Milan because he was an incompetent Duke; Frampul was abandoned by his wife because they had produced no son: the difference is one between the public and the private worlds. To the inn come Lady Frampul and Frances, the Host's daughter, who has inherited the estate. I shall not try to enumerate all the complications of Jonson's presentation, but I should refer you to Harriett Hawkins's excellent article, 'The Idea of a Theater in Jonson's *The New Inn*' in *Renaissance Drama*.[8] And I should remind you that Frank, apparently the Host's son, is disguised as a lady, apparently sister to Frances: this exceeds the kind of incredibility that Shakespeare had long played with and that in *Cymbeline* attained its apogee. Special exaltation, however, is given to Prudence, the maid to Lady Frampul (this in itself is an inversion that we must see, in Elizabethan-Jacobean terms, as particularly 'incredible'), and it is she who commands Lovel, the sister of Lady Frampul, to discourse to her on love and valour. The discourses forthcoming are long and eloquent. At the end the Host reveals his identity, and the appropriate marriages are in view. It is a play full of high sentence, yet not a bit obtuse. That the maid Prudence has so dominating a part brings to mind what Molière was to do later, more light-heartedly, with Dorine in *Tartuffe*, or Shakespeare earlier, and more agonisingly, with Cornwall's First Servant in *Lear*: the mere servant can be the voice of wisdom. These things overturn the notion of 'degree' in *Lear*, and make more discreet fun of it in the Jonson and Molière plays.

Now I wish my Greek were less minimal than it is,

but I suspect that only Aristophanes wrote satiric comedy with such extraordinary verse as Jonson used for a similar purpose. Shakespeare could of course give comparable writing in his comedies when to some extent he took the satiric pressure off, as in Biron's apostrophe to 'women's eyes' in *Love's Labour's Lost* or in Lysander's words in *A Midsummer Night's Dream* – 'So quick bright things come to confusion' (i.i.149) – or plentifully in *As You Like It* and *Twelfth Night*; but only Jonson could give us the full taste of iron along with the splendour. Let us think of Sir Epicure Mammon's speeches, which must not be given as if they were the words of a crass citizen but rather those of a truly ambitious, though gulled man, or of the opening speech of Volpone. Both of these characters speak in a splendidly authoritative way, though they are a dupe and a trickster. Jonson can pull it off in prose too, when Volpone plays the part of Scoto and entices Celia to throw her handkerchief to him. If he fails ultimately to seduce or rape her, he has done it in some measure through this earlier superb playing. It is normally what we dream of, as Coleridge in *Christabel* said, not something to be told. Here it is told, and we rejoice with Volpone that his contrivance has for the moment been successful. Is it not 'incredible' that we rejoice, that we feel disappointed when Bonario rescues her? However bad that makes us, it is what surely happens in our response to the play. And it is what Jonson does with his prose and verse that makes us on this occasion so curiously acquiesce in evil.

But Jonson was a writer of masques as well as of plays. The masque inevitably presents an incredibility. What could be more absurd than a quasi-deification of James's court, a pretence that the whole kingdom was well and that it found its total well-being mirrored in the contemplation of that court? Yet Jonson played that game. A masque came near to its end – at least as far as the text went, for the dances went on much longer – with the appearance or descent of the masquers, those exalted figures. They were not to be resisted in court, though Jonson could present a reverse image of them in his anti-masques and in his ruffians of *Bartholomew Fair*. The masque's 'discovery' presents indeed an antonym of the Aristotelian *anagnorisis*, for it gives us a consciousness of what is in this instance right, not of what is wrong. But in his comedies he does indeed present a true *anagnorisis*, for in *Volpone* all is made anguishedly plain when the Fox wills his own destruction, in *The Alchemist* when the rogue Lovewit brings everything to light even while profiting from it all (even to the point of marrying the nubile Dame Pliant and getting her fortune), in *Bartholomew Fair* when Overdo has to make do with his sudden acknowledging of the emergent truth.

Yet there are further ways in which we can be astonished by Jonson and his comedies. He progressed from a quasi-romantic *The Case is Altered* (we can hardly guess about his earlier lost plays) to *The Sad Shepherd*. He wrote for the boys and for the adult players. He gave the 'humours' a currency which, we have seen, has probably done him harm. He wrote the most successful comedies of the early seventeenth century, yet he went on to bitter and difficult plays that antagonised his audience. He became unpopular, but attached to himself many younger writers who rejoiced to be called 'the sons of Ben,' and influenced not only Caroline and Restoration but some later comedy profoundly. Indeed it was impossible to see Dion Boucicault's *London Assurance*, as it was acted by the Royal Shakespeare Company at the Aldwych in London three years ago, and is still being played, without realising that Jonson was ultimately behind it. Today he has come back to our theatre, for at least his three major plays, and others, I think, will be rediscovered before long.

And the theatre is indeed where he belongs. Shakespeare on occasion, particularly in his histories but sometimes also in comedy and very infrequently in tragedy,
invites us to consider the future that awaits the characters
that we have seen on the stage.[9] Eight of the histories,
being linked plays, necessarily encourage us to envisage
a continuation of England's story: even *Richard III*, the
last of them in relation to its subject matter, tells us to
think of Tudor rule. *As You Like It*, much more self-
enclosed, nevertheless in Jacques' blessing to the four
newly married couples invites our consideration of what
lies ahead for them. And though the tragedies necessarily
have their main emphasis on a greatness destroyed, we
cannot but think of the Roman Empire that was to be
when we come to the final lines of *Antony and Cleopatra*.
In Jonson, on the other hand, nothing of moment lies
beyond the slow death for Volpone and Mosca, an en-
hanced fortune for Lovewit, a supper at Justice Overdo's:
there is not much for the mind to dwell on in any of these
instances. We could feel horror at Volpone's end, but
Jonson undercuts this, as we have seen, by having the
player of his part speak the epilogue. 'He is, after all, an
actor, ready to do it all again,' is our reaction, and our
sense of horror is largely banished. The play is truly over.
Here Jonson is in step with the general movement that
belongs to the comic tradition: the dramatist may incidentally move or perplex, even shock us, but there is a
tidying up, almost a mocking of us for having been so
much taken in. That is part of the 'incredibility' of all
comedy that I spoke of at the beginning of this paper.
Here, it will be understood, the term 'comedy' is used in
relation to the mainstream in drama from Aristophanes
to Shaw and to some extent beyond: sometimes one is
puzzled in contemplating in what dark caves the mainstream is now flowing. Quite of a different order is the
'comedy' that the Middle Ages talked of, that reached its

height in Dante, and that had a fine baroque flowering in the major plays of Calderón. Comedy, in the normal sense of the word, both ancient and modern, does indeed take us in. We know that life as we have experienced it is only partially related to what the comic dramatist offers us; yet we are involved, we respond, sympathise, even hope and fear; then everything is neatly packed away, and we are told, as so splendidly in *Twelfth Night* and *Volpone* and *The Alchemist*, to go home and remember only that we have had an afternoon or evening at the theatre. Of course, we cannot quite do that: the dramatist will have told us too much for us to leave in a totally easy frame of mind. Certainly Christopher Fry has argued that tragedy's blinkers are even narrower,[10] and in this place I shall remark merely that, when we set pen to paper, even the noblest Kind of writing puts limits to us and that to me those of comedy seem more strict.

In any event, the 'incredibility' is not especially Jonson's, though he offers it with major effrontery. The effect, with him as with others, depends in some measure on restriction, both in plot and in character. Jonson had a regard for the so-called 'Unities,' although in the Induction to *Every Man Out of His Humour* he could refuse to give them entire endorsement. When Mitis, the gentle critic, enquires whether the author of the play has seen to it that 'the whole Argument fall within compasse of a dayes businesse' (Induction, 11.240–1), Cordatus, the author's friend, denies that any dramatist should be tied to the ways of his predecessors: pointing out that in the history of ancient drama each writer in turn felt free to make changes on an established pattern, he asserts firmly:

I see not then, but we should enioy the same licence, or free power, to illustrate and heighten our inuention as

*they did; and not bee tyed to those strict and regular
formes, which the nicenesse of a few (who are nothing
but forme) would thrust vpon vs.* [11. 266–70]

Even so, Jonson customarily keeps the place single and
the time short. Yet indeed he crowds them: to get so much
into one place and one day is to defy belief. Now, we
have all probably lived through days that, in retrospect,
seem to contain simply too much to be credited, as I have
elsewhere suggested in connection with Malcolm Lowry's
Under the Volcano.[11] Nevertheless, such days are rare,
and in the theatre, when the theatre uses the comic Kind,
a crowding of events into a narrow compass is primarily
part of the fun, the make-believe. So many visitors to
Lovewit's house within so few hours? A barely inter-
rupted sequence of would-be heirs coming to Volpone's
bed? So many interrelated intrigues on a single day at the
Fair? In our more nearly rational moments we could not
believe in these things, but the magic – or custom, for
magic is its custom – of the theatre gives us licence to
accept. Far from inducing a sense of verisimilitude, the
narrow restriction of time and place in a comedy normally
stretches our capacity for belief. The situation in tragedy
is as complex but quite different, but that is something
we cannot pursue here.

Jonson underlines the restriction of the characters
through his general use of labels for names. It is true that
Face's 'real' name is Jeremy, but we know him as 'Face'
or 'Lungs'; Doll is Common in name as well as habit;
Subtle is only, and magnificently, Subtle. The animal-
names in *Volpone* shut the figures off from us as quasi-
emblems; Celia and Bonario are almost nullified by what
their names suggest; Overdo invites to be overdone.
Because they are so limited by their names, it is extraordinary how involved we can become with them. At the

end, however, the pageant is over, and we banish them all from our hearts, though not from our memories. Did we ever worry over Celia's predicament? Yes, we did, but we do not take any vestige of that home with us, though we shall doubtless remember that Volpone's attempted seduction or rape is quite remarkably presented. It is, by the way, true that some years ago at Stratford-upon-Avon I began to feel more worried about Volpone than about Celia, but that was due to the unfortunate casting of Volpone and the superb casting of Celia. But when the end comes, when, as we have seen, Volpone speaks the Epilogue, none of the characters exists for us any more. We are no longer credulous: we know only that we have seen a great 'show,' which nevertheless has made us feel, in a curious way, more knowledgeable about the human animal. Perhaps for that reason the 'show' given by Nano, Androgyno, and Castrone in the first scene is truly appropriate to the whole action. It is a piece of bitter and fantastical nonsense, having a truth nevertheless of its own. At least, that is how a Jacobean or a twentieth-century man must look back on the ancients: the philosopher's soul has descended into the body of the man-woman fool.

I have suggested that Jonson carried to its limit what is inherent in the 'mainstream' of comedy, urging us to believe when we have difficulty in believing. Yet his ambition did not stay there, though it was in this kind of writing that he did his major work. I have referred briefly to *The New Inn*, a play nearer to Shakespeare's final romances than we could have expected; he did not complete *The Sad Shepherd*, a pastoral which is very different in its effect from either Guarini's *Il Pastor Fido* or Fletcher's *The Faithful Shepherdess*: it has neither the sanguineness of the one nor the discreet mockery of the other; he began to write *The Fall of Mortimer*, which

might have become an important codicil to the plays on
English history that constituted an important achievement of the 1590s. He wrote, of course, two completed
tragedies in *Sejanus* and *Catiline*, splendid and unpopular plays, trying to give to England something nearer to
Seneca, and to the ancient world generally, than had been
previously achieved in the public theatre. But his major
contribution to our drama in English resides in comedy.
There he simultaneously demands and defies belief. That
was Shakespeare's way in comedy too. 'Oh, what nonsense,' we feel obliged to comment, with part of our
minds, when we see *As You Like It* or *Twelfth Night*. Yet
we respond and indeed suffer for a while, at least in
Twelfth Night. Jonson, using a form which approximated
more closely to the Terentian-Plautine pattern, defied us
even further. Suspense, nevertheless, remained wholly in
his hands: he made us anxious to know what was going
to happen to his characters, yet made fun of us in the end
by tidying things up, making us realise it was all only a
matter of 'make-believe.'

Yet he asserted there was something more. We have
already seen that in the Dedication to the 'Two Universities' prefixed to *Volpone* he insisted that his purpose
was didactic: to him that has done evil, so shall it be
rendered, he implied. Again let us remember Volpone's
speaking of the Epilogue (which is, in a minor key, repeated when Face speaks the Epilogue to *The Alchemist*),
which negates the whole matter. Lessing argued that,
although perhaps comedy never cured anyone of his
vices, it could strengthen a man in his present condition
of health.[12] Frankly, I doubt it: I do not think we go away
from any of Jonson's comedies with a fortification of our
assumed healthy condition. We are indeed optimistic if
we do. Rather we say: 'This is incredible, but it is perhaps
uncomfortably right; perhaps we are really as bad as this;

perhaps this is how, like Lovewit, we might for a time get away with it, how, like Volpone, we might have to endure a punishment for incurring the wrath of a corrupt society, how, like Justice Overdo, we might have to swallow down our ambition to put things right.' But in the theatre we are not much anguished. In reading, indeed, we may well be. Jonson belongs to the theatre, where these troubling thoughts are dissipated when the actor playing Volpone speaks the Epilogue, when Lovewit has brought it off (as we should all like to do), when Overdo has at least a communal supper to look forward to.

Yet, when we come away from the theatre – and Bacon, you will remember, said it was not good to remain there too long – we are perhaps anxious. We know that we cannot be so fortunate as Lovewit, that the ending of Volpone may await us, or at least the humiliation of Justice Overdo. The incredible becomes the truth, and it is Face's, or Volpone's, or Overdo's, in addition to Lovewit's, ending that compels our incredulous belief.

NOTES

1 *The Prose Works of Sir Philip Sidney*, ed. Albert Feuillerat (reprinted Cambridge 1963), III, 38
2 Cf. *The Two Gentlemen of Verona*, New Arden edition (London 1969), lx–lxi
3 John W. Draper, *The Humors and Shakespeare's Characters* (Durham, NC, 1945)
4 Quotations from Jonson are from *Ben Jonson*, ed. C.H. Herford and P. and E. Simpson, 11 vols (Oxford 1925–52)
5 Quotations from Marston are from *The Plays of John Marston*, ed. H.H. Wood (Edinburgh 1934)
6 Ibid., I, 230
7 Cf. *The John Fletcher Plays* (London 1962), 156–7
8 'The Idea of a Theater in Jonson's *The New Inn*,' *Renaissance Drama*, IX (1966), 205–26

9 Cf. 'Shakespeare and the Idea of the Future,' *University of Toronto Quarterly*, xxxv (April 1966), 213–28
10 'Comedy,' *The Adelphi* (November 1950), 27–9
11 *The Dramatist's Experience with Other Studies in Literary Theory*, London 1970, 106
12 *The Laocoon and Other Prose Writings of Lessing*, tr. W.B. Rönnfeldt, The Scott Library (London n.d.), 210

JONSON AND
THE LOATHÈD STAGE

JONAS A. BARISH

Some years ago, when post-romantic prejudice was at last on the wane, and Jonson was first beginning to be studied sympathetically, U.M. Ellis-Fermor made a provocative comment in her book on the Jacobean drama. 'As an artist and as a man,' she wrote, 'Ben Jonson was originally non-dramatic; at no time did he dramatize himself and it was only with some difficulty that he dramatized anything else. ... There is, as it were, a deeply inherent non-dramatic principle in him.'[1] As phrased, this observation seems open to question in certain ways. Jonson surely did dramatize things and persons other than himself, with such exceptional energy that it sometimes seems as instinctual as breathing, and it might be argued on *a priori* grounds that far from never dramatizing himself, he could hardly have done otherwise, that a playwright can only give voice to what is already inside him, however he may ventriloquize it and project it onto other imagined creatures. Still, it is hard not to feel, at times, that Jonson's vocation goes against the grain; it seems to arouse severe inner resistances. Instead of 'a deeply inherent non-dramatic principle,' however, I would prefer to speak of a deeply rooted antitheatricalism. In common with many of us, Jonson's attitude toward the theatre was split by contradictions. He belongs, in spirit, among a galaxy of talented playwrights who at a given moment in their careers have seen their whole enterprise as hollow, and proceeded to renounce it, or else reform it, in more or less spectacular and theatrical fashion. In this company would go Racine, Calderón, Rousseau, and even Plato, if the tradition is correct according to which he wrote comedies as a young man, not to mention such insignificant Englishmen as Stephen Gosson and Anthony Munday. Other playwrights seem to maintain an endlessly unstable and conflicted relation with the stage. Eugene O'Neill, for example, registered repeated dismay at what he scathingly called the 'show-shop' of the theatre, and recorded his sense of betrayal at what actors, including the most gifted and dedicated actors, made of the characters he had forged in the silence of his imagination. Even in such born men of the theatre as Shakespeare and Molière, we find moments of deep suspicion toward theatricality as a form of behaviour in the world.

Jonson is not, therefore, to be thought of as a fluke, but as one in whom a familiar ambivalence remains unresolved, and in whom it produced certain stresses and prompted certain accommodations. To some extent it helped shape his career; it helps account for the character of his successes and the accent of his failures. One finds Jonson at loggerheads with his calling in numerous ways: in his prickly relations with his audiences and his caustic view of the stage practice of his day, in his critical theories about the drama and also in his larger ethical and philosophical assumptions. Familiar though these attitudes of his may be, it is perhaps worth rehearsing them again in orderly fashion, and trying to set them in proper relation to each other.

The first and most obvious thing to say is that Jonson, despite a life-time of writing for the stage, never arrived at a comfortable *modus vivendi* with his audiences. His feelings toward them ranged from gingerly to stormy, and by the time he had been at the job of pleasing them for a few years, he had formed some fairly devastating conclusions. Playgoers, he believed, frequented the theatre in order to parade their fine clothes and gape at those of their neighbours – to make spectacles of themselves, in fact, and so compete with the play. Or they came clamouring for more of the same empty, noisy amusements that had always diverted them in the past: plays filled with shrieks and battles, plays with devils, plays with clowns, and the like. Whatever strained their attention or swerved from stereotype they would 'censure' in boorish ways, turning aside with rude remarks, rising noisily from their places to create a disturbance, or even addressing disruptive remarks to the players. To entertain such audiences was to have to cope with them, to devise stratagems to combat their apathy and circumvent their prejudices. Jonson seems to have thought of the good audience as a kind of jury, assembled to render a verdict on a work of art.[2] He asked of it the impartiality appropriate to a court of law rather than the quick emotionality of fellow sharers in a human experience. Alternatively, he thought of it as a panel of tasters scrupulously assaying the quality of the cuisine.[3] In neither of these capacities did the audiences he knew inspire much confidence. Jonson's canon, we note, contains no *As You Like It*s or *What You Will*s, no plays in which the theatregoers are invited to write their own menu. The closest thing to it would be *Bartholomew Fair*, with its sardonic indenture between poet and pit, in which each side, as in an adversary proceeding, agrees to waive certain claims in return for certain concessions. Only by dint of wary bargaining do the two parties manage to reach a guarded understanding for the duration of the afternoon.

On behalf of this corrupted audience, but without its consent, Jonson repudiated nearly all the popular dramatic genres of the day: romance comedy, revenge tragedy, chronicle history, Marlovian tragedy of ambition. All these, in his view, offended nature because they exaggerated. They traded in monsters and chimeras instead of recognizable human types. They bruised the ear with 'furious vociferation,' or fatigued the eye with '*scenicall* strutting.'[4] Taken literally, Jonson's prescriptions of 'truth' and 'nature' would have forbidden even the kind of heightening he himself freely practised, not to speak of the grotesques of *Volpone* or the wild improbabilities of *Epicene*. When it came to stagecraft, he rejected with equal vehemence all the varieties of theatrical claptrap most cherished by Elizabethan audiences: fireworks, thunder, and ordnance, the raising of ghosts from the cellarage and lowering of gods from the hut. In the course of his feud with Inigo Jones, Jonson also ridiculed such newer and more esoteric wonders as the *machina versatilis*, or turning device, and the *machina ductilis*, or tractable scene, both of them among the admired playthings of the court theatre. One common factor in these dislikes, as W.A. Armstrong has pointed out, is that 'they were all directed against scenes, lights and machines which *moved* before the spectators' eyes' and were hence 'most likely to distract attention from the spoken word.'[5] More may be at stake here, however, than simple attentiveness. Other playwrights managed to preserve the primacy of the spoken word without sacrificing the pleasures of spectacle. Somewhere in Jonson there lurks a puritanical uneasiness about pleasure itself, and also a distrust of movement, which connects with what we shall presently see to be an ideal of stasis in the moral and ontological realm. But whatever exists in time, and unfolds in time, and utilizes human actors, must also involve motion as one of its mainsprings. To banish motion, to attempt to arrest or disguise it by ruling out the devices of stagecraft that exploit it, is in a sense to deny the intrinsically kinetic nature of the theatrical medium.

Jonson himself would not have countenanced the suggestion that he was attacking the theatre in its essence. He would have claimed to be reforming it, removing its excrescences, bringing it back to nature after orgies of extravagance. But his reform aims precisely to detheatricalize the theatre, to strip it of just those attributes which, in the eyes of most of its votaries, made it theatre in the first place: not only its gaudiness, its bustle and splendour, but also – what Jonson deeply objected to – its licentious ways with time and place, and its sovereign command of the astounding and the marvellous. Samuel Beckett has initiated a somewhat similar reform in our own day, trying to renew an art that has rotted in its own pomp by stripping away all theatrical tinsel so as to get back to the primitive basis of a pair of characters playing on a few square feet of unadorned board. Beckett goes further than Jonson in one respect; he also eliminates all luxuriance of speech. Jonson's answer to the stage sensationalism of his day was a more highly wrought rhetoric, and we may allow this to be a genuinely theatrical answer, even if his contemporaries did not always agree. One of his authentic masterpieces, *Sejanus*, was hissed from the stage because of the excesses of its verbiage, yet when Jonson sat down to write a second tragedy for the same troupe a few years later, far from conceding anything to the preferences of his audiences, he defiantly administered a double dose of what they had already once spat out, as though to coerce them into swallowing his medicine even if they found it unpalatable, on the pre-

31

sumption that he knew better than they what was good for them.

Theatrical performance remained, throughout his career, a hazard for Jonson, fraught with the perils of rejection and trauma. His ambivalence about it emerges plainly in his attitude toward the printing of his plays. As early as 1600 the title-page of *Every Man Out of His Humor* informs us that this is 'The Comicall Satyre of EVERY MAN OUT OF HIS HUMOR, AS IT WAS FIRST COMPOSED by the AUTHOR B.I. *Containing more than hath been Publickely Spoken or Acted.* With the severall Character of every Person.' Now this unusual legend at the same time announces an innovation and issues a challenge. Standard title-page salesmanship during the 1590s had stressed the identity of the play as printed with that of the play as acted. Dramatic texts aimed to capitalize on theatrical successes by offering authentic transcripts of what had been well received by audiences. A play was published 'as acted by' or 'as played by' such and such a company, or as 'sundrie time shewed upon Stages,' or even 'most stately shewed,' or as 'privately acted,' or as 'Played before the Queen's most excellent Majesty.' The 1594 quarto of *A Knack to Know a Knave* advertises proudly that it is 'Newlie set foorth, as it hath sundrie tymes bene played by ED. ALLEN and his Companie. With KEMPS applauded Merrimentes,' while the 1597 quarto of *Romeo and Juliet* calls attention to the fact that the play has been 'often (with great applause) plaid publiquely, by the right Honourable the L. of Hunsdon his Servants.'[6]

Jonson completely overturns this custom. Instead of promising us that the printed version will conform to the acted one, he assures us that it will not. It will be 'as first composed by the author' – presumably superior to, and in any case different from the acted version, about which he leaves us in the dark, not even mentioning the name of the company. Moreover he casts a lure for the browser by first including and then pointing to 'the severall Character of every Person,' a series of quasi-Theophrastean sketches which could only interest a reader and could not have found any place in performance. Jonson, clearly, is thinking of the play now as a reading experience rather than a theatrical experience, as a literary entity, with rules of its own that dispense it from such purely theatrical constraints as that on length: the text runs to something like 4500 lines, substantially longer than *Hamlet*. Print, again, offered the chance to expatiate on critical questions, to debate disputed points, affix postscripts, and append emendations. The original ending of *Every Man Out of His Humour* having offended because it contained an impersonation of the queen, Jonson rewrote it, but in the printed text he preserved the original finale along with the altered one, and supplied a learned apology addressed to the 'right-ei'd and solide *Reader*' (III,602).

Analogous considerations, most likely, govern the two states of the text of *Cynthia's Revels*. The quarto would seem to represent an acting version – certainly it is by far the tighter and more concise of the two – while the folio either reverts to an enormous urtext from which the acting script was carved out, or else represents a gigantic expansion of the acted text for inclusion in the later volume. For the folio version of *Poetaster*, again, Jonson seems to have composed an entire new scene, the most striking feature of which is its total unsuitability for performance. The scene, a close paraphrase of a satire of Horace, does nothing to accommodate itself to the dramatic context. It makes no reference to characters or events of the play, but on the other hand it does mention numerous characters and events quite alien to the play, because they are mentioned in Horace. Of the two speakers of the scene, one is Horace, but the Horace of history rather than the Horace of the play, with no traces of his dramatic self, and the other is Horace's colourless interlocutor

Trebatius, who has otherwise nothing at all to do with *Poetaster*. As a contribution to literature, as an excursus on the theory of satire, as an exercise in translation, the scene possesses distinct interest. But coming as part of the dramatic continuum of *Poetaster* it forms a most ill-fitting and unwelcome intrusion. For both these plays, then, when it came to putting them into definitive form for the volume he designed as a monument, Jonson chose to introduce — or reintroduce — extensive literary embellishments that seriously injure them as stage pieces. Even the revised *Every Man in His Humour*, despite its greater richness of texture, strikes one as a more bookish object than its quarto original. The revisions, most of them additions, tend to encrust and at times to encumber with detail what was previously a sparer, sharper pattern of action.

But the very collecting of his plays into the 1616 folio testifies to Jonson's impatience with the fragility of the stage, and his desire to commit his 'works' — significantly so named — to a more lasting medium. In this respect he forms a sharp contrast to Marston, who in the foreword to *The Malcontent* apologizes for printing his play at all, on the grounds that it does not truly exist apart from its theatrical embodiment. '*Onely one thing afflicts me,*' he declares mournfully, '*to thinke that Scaenes invented, meerely to be spoken, should be inforcively published to be read.*'[7] Again in the address prefixed to *The Fawne* he alleges unwillingness and pleads necessity: '*If any shall wonder why I print a Comedie, whose life rests much in the Actors voice, Let such know, that it cannot avoide publishing: let it therefore stand with good excuse, that I have been my owne setter out.*'[8] The burden of proof, in Marston's view, is thus on the playwright who would transfer his comedies, meant for the stage, into print. For Jonson, on the other hand, the actor's voice — not to speak of the public's ear — constituted an unpredictable and

untrustworthy element over which he had too little control; print offered an escape into a stabler medium. In
preface and dedication and apologetical epistle he appeals
to readers over the heads of playhouse audiences. The
latter cannot truly measure the worth of what is offered
them; they are bent on instant gratifications of a kind he
has little wish to supply, and are, in the nature of things,
prone to be swayed by opinion rather than reason.
Readers, simply by virtue of literacy, possess a certain
minimum of knowledge and discipline. In addition, they
are removed from the passions of the playhouse. They
can ponder, instead of blindly reacting, and so bring cool
heads and sound judgments to the act of evaluation. The
end result of such considerations is to make the printed
script rather than the live performance the final authority;
the play moves formally into the domain of literature.
Jonson makes this clear in the prefatory remarks to
Sejanus and *Catiline*, when he defends these plays not
against the discontented groundlings at the Globe, not
against the charges of tedium, insufficient action, and so
forth, that had actually caused them to fail, but against
what he fancies *might* be said in their reproof by learned
commentators steeped in Aristotle and conversant with
the erudite debates on tragedy. *Sejanus* lacks 'a proper
Chorus' and does not adhere to 'the strict Lawes of *Time*'
('To the Readers,' ll. 7–8); *Catiline*, despite *'all noise of
opinion,'* is *'a legitimate Poeme'* (Dedication, ll. 6–7).
Jonson is not interested in vindicating the theatrical
viability of his plays, but in validating them as literature,
as correct dramatic poems, from pedantic interpreters on
the right. And as he appeals to readers to mend the hasty
reactions of spectators, so at times he invokes posterity
to correct the errors of his contemporaries, thus aiming
at a level of disinterested judgment unattainable in his
own day even in well-disposed readers.

It is no surprise, then, to discover Jonson more passionately concerned with the fate of his plays in the printing-house than any other dramatic author of the period. For the 1616 folio he exercised an unprecedentedly close surveillance over the whole process, supplying corrected copy, reading proof while the volume was in press, and (at least for the earlier plays) entering scores of minute revisions in order to clarify his intentions or enhance the typographical impact of the presentation.

As with the publishing of the plays, so with that of the masques; the purpose is 'to redeeme them as well from Ignorance, as Envie, two common evills' (*Masque of Blackness*, ll. 12–14). Here the discrepancy between print and performance widens, since the very essence of the masque lay in its occasional nature and its absolute reliance on spectacle. Far from attempting to deny it this character, Jonson at first puts his whole weight behind it, justifying the cost and sumptuousness of the form as an expression of kingly magnificence, and going to great lengths to make the printed texts recreate as far as possible the brilliant scenic effects of Inigo Jones. With Jones, also, he worked to devise spectacular effects that would function as vehicles of meaning, and could not be written off as mere decoration. But even as he bent his energies to unifying the form and reconciling its disparate elements, Jonson in the depths of his mind preserved a firm belief in the paramountcy of poetry. Spectacle, however splendid, however central and expressive, could never be more than the 'carkasse' of an organism whose 'spirit' lay in the verses. These terms, from *The Masque of Blackness* (l. 8) recur, slightly varied and with renewed emphasis, in the foreword to *Hymenaei*:

It is a noble and just advantage, that the things subjected to understanding *have of those which are objected to* sense, *that the one sort are but momentarie, and meerely taking; the other impressing, and lasting: Else the glorie*

36

of all these solemnities *had perish'd like a blaze, and gone out, in the* beholders *eyes. So short-liv'd are the* bodies *of all things, in comparison of their* soules. *And though* bodies *oft-times have the ill luck to be sensually preferr'd, they find afterwards, the good fortune (when* soules *live) to be utterly forgotten.* [ll. 1–10]

As carcass to spirit, so body to soul. In the poetic kernel of the masque lies its abiding essence, in the theatrical vesture only a disposable shell. The poetry addresses itself to the understanding, that faculty which Jonson consistently exalts over its coarser companion 'sense,' and to which he appeals as the highest faculty he can hope for in a reader or spectator. Sense, indeed, he informs us elsewhere, we should strive to make our 'slave' ('Epode,' ll. 17–18). By the time we reach *Pleasure Reconciled to Virtue* Jonson's interest in the spectacular side of the masque has unmistakably waned. The text, instead of lovingly dwelling on the details of costume and décor, actually omits some of the most striking visual effects remarked by other observers: the richly decorated front curtain, the pantomime battle between Hercules and Antaeus, the reappearance of the goddess Virtue. 'Far from being' – as it would have been earlier – 'the record of a particular production on a particular evening in 1618, the text seems almost to testify to the irrelevance of the spectator's experience.'[9] Moreover, when members of the audience criticized the entertainment, as they did, they found fault with it not on visual but on poetic grounds. Jonson had trained them to view such shows through his own eyes, and to apply to them his own canons of dramatic poetry.[10]

Despite, then, the innovative energy with which Jonson tackled the aesthetic problems of the masque, despite his efforts to forge apt and expressive devices of stage spectacle, he persisted, in the depths of his mind, in

holding the spectacular side of the masque in low esteem.
Speaking in the *Discoveries* of the quest for magnificence, he reminds us that 'Wee covet superfluous things;
when it were more honour for us, if wee could contemne
necessary.'

Have not I seene the pompe of a whole Kingdome, and
what a forraigne King could bring hither also to make
himself gaz'd, and wonder'd at, laid forth as it were to
the shew, and vanish all away in a day? And shall that
which could not fill the expectation of few houres, enter-
taine, and take up our whole lives? when even it appear'd
as superfluous to the Possessors, as to me that was a
Spectator. The bravery was shewne, it was not possess'd;
while it boasted it self, it perish'd. [ll. 1387–9, 1404–12]

Jonson may or may not here be thinking specifically of
a masque, but it is hardly to be doubted that behind the
description lie his long years of apprenticeship to court
spectacles, and his settled conviction of their wasteful-
ness. Welcoming a newcomer to the Tribe of Ben, he
distinguishes between true friendships and flimsy ones,
between 'Such as are square, wel-tagde, and permanent,'
and those 'built with Canvasse, paper, and false lights, /
As are the Glorious Scenes, at the great sights' (63–6).
Here the masque becomes an express symbol for what is
fleeting, trumped-up, and inauthentic, the antithesis of
everything valuable and lasting.

One ground, evidently, for Jonson's distrust of both
play and masque is the inherent impermanence of both
forms. Jonson belongs in a Christian-Platonic-Stoic tradition that finds value embodied in what is immutable
and unchanging, and tends to dismiss as unreal whatever is past and passing and to come. What endures, for
him, has substance; what changes reveals itself thereby
as illusory. His non-dramatic poems recur repeatedly to
the ideal of the unmoved personality, the soul that can

sustain itself in virtue when all is flux around it.[11] Men are praised if they can preserve their singleness of mind amid the distractions of the world, their serenity of spirit amid its turbulence. The Earl of Pembroke, in a Senecan paraphrase, is lauded for his constancy in goodness, for being one 'whose noblêsse keeps one stature still, / And one true posture, though besieg'd with ill' ('To William Earle of Pembroke,' ll. 13–14). Similarly with Lady Katherine Aubigny; it is her firmness of temper that makes her exemplary: '*Madame*, be bold to use this truest glasse: / Wherein, your forme, you still the same shall finde; / Because nor it can change, nor such a minde' ('To Katherine Lady Aubigny,' ll. 122–4). Here the stasis aspired to by the poet, and achieved in the finality of his poem, mirrors the still perfection of its idealized subject. Earlier in the same poem, as often in Jonsonian verse, the satiric vision momentarily gains the ascendant; we glimpse the social turmoil eschewed by the lady, the temptations against which she remains steadfast:

> *... wisely you decline your life,*
> *Farre from the maze of custome, error, strife,*
> *And keepe an even, and unalter'd gaite;*
> *...*
> *Which though the turning world may dis-esteeme,*
> *Because that studies spectacles, and showes,*
> *And after varyed, as fresh objects goes,*
> *Giddie with change, and therefore cannot see*
> *Right, the right way: yet must your comfort bee*
> *Your conscience, and not wonder, if none askes*
> *For truthes complexion, where they all weare maskes.*
> [ll. 59–70]

One catches a hint of masque terminology here. The 'turning world' recalls the revolving microcosm of *Hymenaei*, only now the whole world – masquers and beholders together – has become a *machina versatilis*. Jonson seems to condemn the taste for novelty and the thirst for change independently, as if they constituted separate but related vices, just as on another occasion he makes it more of a sin when vices 'do not tary in a place,' but shift about.

In the *Discoveries* the craze for playgoing appears along with other frivolous pursuits as a symbol of childishness and the abdication of judgment on the part of grown men:

What a deale of cold busines doth a man mis-spend the better part of life in! in scattering complements, *tendring* visits, *gathering and venting* newes, *following* Feasts *and* Playes, *making a little winter-love in a darke corner.*
[ll. 56–9]

Certainly the most avid playgoers among Jonson's *dramatis personae* rank among his most perfect fools: Fabian Fitzdottrel, of *The Devil is an Ass*, who hastens to the Blackfriars in order to strut in his new cloak, and Bartholomew Cokes, of *Bartholomew Fair*, scarcely able to distinguish the reality of dolls, puppets, and gingerbread men from that of live human beings.

In 'An Epistle to a Friend, to perswade him to the Warres,' Jonson urges his friend to keep himself unsoiled by the baseness of his surroundings, and to maintain his calm of spirit: 'That whatsoever face thy fate puts on, / Thou shrinke or start not, but be alwayes one' (185–6). Fate, like an actor, resourceful in disguise, changes countenance and tries to ensnare the good man, but the good man himself remains 'always one,' always himself, in the face of all vicissitudes. Such activity as he does engage in, such energy as he does put forth, is exerted to preserve his immobility. Immobility is to be fought for; change is to be resisted. In the dialogue of the One and the Many in the Jonsonian cosmos, it is the

Many that must be put to flight, and the One that must finally triumph.

Change not only betokens instability; in the ethical realm it often betokens deceit, and deceit expresses itself characteristically through change. In 'An Epistle to Master Arthur Squib' we learn that 'Deceit is fruitfull. Men have Masques and nets, / But these with wearing will themselves unfold: / They cannot last. No lie grew old' (ll. 18–20). Only the truth survives; lies perish, and that which perishes is compounded of lies. The same message meets us more prosaically in the *Discoveries*, where the terms are such as to suggest an indictment of poetry itself. 'Nothing is lasting that is fain'd; it will have another face then it had, ere long: As *Euripides* saith, *no lye ever growes old*' (ll. 540–2). Even the invocation of the august name of Euripides cannot obscure the hint that the poet's own most hallowed talent, the one that sets the seal on his special status, his 'faining,' is coming under fire.

Now the bias against change, the allegiance to silence, stasis, and immobility carry with them an implied bias against the theatre which occasionally erupts into more explicit form. Jonson's fierce epigram 'On the Townes Honest Man,' apparently written against Inigo Jones, portrays the title personage making his way in the world by miming.

> At every meale, where it doth dine, or sup,
>   The cloth's no sooner gone, but it gets up
> And, shifting of it's faces, doth play more
>   Parts, than th'Italian could doe, with his dore.
> Acts old Iniquitie, and in the fit
>   Of miming, gets th'opinion of a wit. [ll. 23–8]

There is no question here about 'it's' talent for its degrading feats – it is a past master of them – nor is any gloss needed to underline Jonson's contempt for the parasite who pays for his dinner by doing tricks of mimicry. When we turn to the plays we find that in them Jonson does not shed his antitheatrical bias. Rather, he builds it in; he makes the plays critiques of the instability they incarnate. The plays show us change as something to be shunned, by presenting us with foolish characters determined to embrace it. Discontented with themselves, barely able to credit their own reality, addicted to appearances and externals, they compensate by trying to impose some mimic version of themselves on their fellows, and characteristically they resort to theatrical means to make their way. They fall into two well-recognized groups: the gulls, who witlessly parrot their social or intellectual superiors, and so disavow whatever is true in themselves in favour of some forged identity, and the rascals, engaged in various games of pretence, in plays-within-plays which have as object the gulling of the gulls. Thus with Mosca's aid Volpone plays sick to dupe his heirs, plays the mountebank to entice Celia, plays the commendatore to needle his victims once he has gulled them, and teaches Voltore to enact a scene of demonic possession in the courtroom. Subtle, Face, and Doll play an extensive repertory of roles to hoodwink their clients: learned doctor, saintly philosopher, professor of quarrelling, gentleman's servant, laboratory assistant, suburb captain, lord's sister, Queen of Faery. Less malignly Truewit plays the solicitous friend to Morose, orchestrating the confusions of the wedding feast, fashioning the quarrel between the two foolish knights (before a carefully prepared audience), and finally planning, rehearsing, and executing the parody of legal procedure that terminates Morose's matrimonial misadventures. The degree to which Truewit may be allowed to stand as the authorial spokesman in the play suggests the degree to which, in this play, theatricality is accepted as a necessary evil. For the most part, those who engage in deceit may be fruitful, but they are also doomed to exposure. This may explain why Surly, the one honest man in a nest of knaves, loses his just reward, the hand of Dame Pliant. He has chosen to pit disguise against disguise, to change into a Spanish Don as Subtle has changed into an alchemist, and the result is that the fruits of deceit are ravished from his grasp. On the other hand, the relatively inert and inexpert theatricality of the gulls in all the plays works to create a mimetic hierarchy which cuts across the moral hierarchy. We recognize the greater moral culpability of the rascals even as we find ourselves drawn to them in admiring fascination.

The plays, in any case, present a world in which sharpsters try to cozen dullards by means of theatrical humbug, and the dullards try to foist some implausible mask of themselves onto the world. Imposture, thus, takes the form of theatricality. In more didactic vein we sometimes find in Jonsonian comedy an explicit equation between metamorphosis of the self and moral vacuity. In the quarto of *Every Man in His Humour*, Bobadil is scathingly referred to as 'signior *Pithagoras*, he that's al manner of shapes' (III.iv.174–5), by his arch-enemy, a character ultimately named Downright, whose property it is to be as stubbornly himself at all times as it is Bobadil's to lack an authentic self, and whose mission it is to expose Bobadil as a braggart. In *Every Man Out of His Humour* we meet the rascally pseudo-soldier Cavalier Shift, alias Whiff, alias Apple-John, whose self-proclaimed omnicompetence ends with his too being shown up as a swaggerer and coward. And *Cynthia's Revels* brings us acquainted with Amorphus, 'a travailer, one so made out of the mixture and shreds of formes, that himselfe is truly deform'd' (II.iii.85–7). Amorphus, like

43

Bobadil and Shift, is arraigned for the crime of wilful self-betrayal, for piecing together a factitious identity from the scraps of those he has met in his travels.

All these characters, as well as less talented, more monochrome gulls like Stephen or Fungoso or Asotus, in the same three plays, may serve as emblems to one of Jonson's most familiar dicta in the *Discoveries*:

I have *considered, our whole life is like a* Play: *wherein every man, forgetfull of himselfe, is in travaile with expression of another. Nay, wee so insist in imitating others, as wee cannot (when it is necessary) returne to our selves: like Children, that imitate the vices of* Stammerers *so long, till at last they become such* ... [ll. 1093–8]

What this statement signals is not only that men too often walk their daily rounds as if they were acting on stages, but that this is a self-negating, self-destructive way to live. By their persistence in mimicry they are stunting their own possibilities for self-realization. The sole characters who succeed in avoiding this fate, in transcending the evils of their taste for mimicry, are those, like Brainworm, whose antics spring purely from play, on the success of which neither their economic survival nor their sense of their own reality depends.

Two passages in *Cynthia's Revels* embroider lavishly on the ills of change and mimicry. The first consists of a satirical diatribe spoken by Crites, the authorial spokesman. In the manner of much verse satire of the period, Crites recounts a vision or dream he has had of the hangers-on who infest the court, and compose 'a pageant, fashion'd like a court.' The striking thing about this pageant is its particoloured appearance. It has no distinct shape or hue of its own, but remains 'diffus'd ... painted, pyed, and full of rainbow straines.' Its individual members share the same unfixed, variegated character, as we discover in Crites's denunciatory portraits of them: the self-important great man, basking haughtily in his 'state,' attended by 'mimiques, jesters, pandars, parasites'; the 'mincing marmoset,' all clothes and grimaces and starched formality; the venal taker-in of bribes and refuser of honest suits. As the bribe-taker proceeds along,

> With him there meets some subtle PROTEUS, one
> Can change, and varie with all formes he sees;
> Be any thing but honest; serves the time;
> Hovers betwixt two factions, and explores
> The drifts of both ... [III.iv.42–26]

That the Proteus can be 'any thing but honest' is almost a tautology. If he were honest, he would not be a Proteus; the two conditions mutually exclude one another.

Crites goes on to recollect a comic scene played by a group of foolish courtiers, all engaged in perfecting their parts as courtly lovers: the neophyte primping and rehearsing his speech beforehand, 'like an unperfect *prologue*, at third musike'; another who 'sweares / His *Scene* of courtship over,' and strikes poses for his mistress; another who acts in more strenuous mode, overwhelming her with ridiculous gallantries, extravagating in vows and kisses; and one, finally, who 'onely comes in for a *mute*: / Divides the *act* with a dumbe shew, and *exit*.' When the suitors are done, it is their mistresses' turn. 'Then must the ladies laugh, straight comes their *Scene*, / A sixt times worse confusion then the rest' (III.iv.4–74). So, implicitly, in the posturing and attitudinizing and protean shifting of these characters, and explicitly in the theatrical images, we find acting used as a synonym for what is false, affected, and empty. Worth, in the Jonsonian universe, as in that of his Stoic guides, is virtually defined as an inner and hence an invisible quality. Whatever can be too readily theatricalized lacks genuineness and substance. We see this comically spelled out again in the scene in which Amorphus tries to coach his oafish pupil Asotus to approach, address, and pay court to his mistress. The fact that courtliness can be conceived in such mechanical terms, that it can be codified into lessons and practised like acrobatics, tells us all we need to know of its meaning for the characters in the play.

The follies of change appear strikingly exemplified in a character named Phantaste, one of the frivolous nymphs who have desertlessly wormed their way into the purlieus of the court. Phantaste proposes, as a game, that she and her companions imagine whom they would most like to be turned into, if given the chance. Her companions prove to have rather dry imaginations. All that the old bawd, Moria, can think of to wish for is to be 'a wisewoman, and know all the secrets of court, citie, and countrie' (iv.i.140–2). Philautia, or self-love, is too pleased with herself as she already is to be much interested in changing; all she craves is more sovereignty. Most of the scene is given over to the musings of Phantaste, who envisages, as her ideal, an endless cycle of shifting identities.

(mee thinkes) I should wish my selfe all manner of creatures. Now, I would bee an empresse; and by and by a dutchesse; then a great ladie of state; then one of your miscelany madams; then a waiting-woman, then your cittizens wife; then a course countrey gentlewoman; then a deyrie maide; then a shepheards lasse; then an empresse againe, or the queene of fayries: And thus I would proove the vicissitudes, and whirle of pleasures, about, and againe.

This gives us, in stylized form, the insatiable thirst for pleasure that seems automatically to lead to a life of perpetual change. Phantaste's revery puts into systematic and as it were aesthetic form the compulsive flitting about among distractions that already constitutes her existence, and her state of mind. 'As I were a shepheardesse,' she proceeds,

*I would bee pip'd and sung too; as a deyrie wench, I would
dance at may-poles, and make sillabubbes; As a countrey
gentlewoman, keep a good house, and come up to terme,
to see motions; As a cittizens wife, bee troubled with a
jealous husband, and put to my shifts; (others miseries
should bee my pleasures) As a waiting-woman, I would
taste my ladies delights to her; As a* miscellany *madame*
*invent new tyres, and goe visite courtiers; As a great
ladie, lye a bed, and have courtiers visite mee; As a dutchesse, I would keepe my state: and as an empresse, I'ld
doe any thing. And, in all these shapes, I would ever bee
follow'd with th'affections of all that see mee.* [IV.i.171–
91]

One noteworthy feature of this daydream is that the individual vignettes in it seem innocent enough. There is
nothing corrupt or culpable about a shepherdess wishing
to be piped and sung to: nothing could be more decorous,
or classical. A milkmaid would not have to be ashamed
of dancing at maypoles and making sillabubs, or a country
gentlewoman of keeping a good house. It is true that
Phantaste leans toward pastime rather than honest
labour, but the pastimes themselves are mostly harmless ones. What is not harmless is the total vision, the
whirligig of metamorphoses which leave no room for a
fixed responsible self.

Metamorphic fantasies, it need hardly be insisted on,
play a key role in Volpone's advances to Celia. He plies
her not only with palpable jewels and the promise of
edible delights, but with the inducement of perpetual
variety in love, the prospect of an endless charade in
which the two will act characters out of history, out of
geography, and out of Ovid's *Metamorphoses*. Similarly,

in the *Epigrams*, the degenerate sensuality of Sir Volup-
tuous Beast takes the form of a search for unusual ways
to arouse and appease his lust; his new wife must learn
to fit herself to the 'varied shapes' of his appetite. And
so for Sir Epicure Mammon, expecting a renewal of youth
from the elixir; he promises Doll Common 'a perpetuitie
/ Of life, and lust.' Like Celia, Doll will have a 'wardrobe, / Richer than *Natures*, still, to change thy selfe, /
And vary oftener, for thy pride, then shee: / Or *Art*, her
wise, and almost-equall servant' (IV.i.166–9). One target
of Jonson's antitheatricalism appears here with particular
emphasis: the fixation on clothes as a source of pleasure
and a basis of identity. Sir Epicure, preoccupied with his
visions of sensual sport, harbours the illusion that a
'wardrobe, / Richer then *Natures*' will open the door to
endless transformations of the self; he and his partner
will moult identities, as it were, and experience well-worn
pleasures as if for the first time. The same wish, for transformation through costume, appears expressed ironically
by Morose, when he tests Epicene by pretending that he
expects her to surpass the other beauties of the court in
variety and modishness of dress:

heare me, faire lady, I doe also love to see her, whom I
shall choose for my heicfar, to be the first and principall
in all fashions; praecede all the dames at court, by a fort-
night; have her counsell of taylors, linneners, lace-
women, embroyderers, and sit with 'hem sometimes twise
a day, upon French intelligences; and then come foorth,
varied like Nature, or oftener then she, and better, by the
helpe of Art, her aemulous servant.
[*Epicene*, II.v.68–75]

Jonson seems to have felt all clothes to be in some sense
disguises. Certainly he saw excessive attachment to them
as a mark of triviality, an addiction to what is inessential

and transitory, as well as a futile and hence perverse attempt to rival nature. Some of his characters display a positively morbid obsession with them. Nick Stuffe, the tailor in *The New Inn*, when he makes a new gown for a lady, uses it to act out a cherished fantasy: he dresses his wife in the commissioned finery, carries her in a coach to an inn, and there throws her down upon a bed. The fact that she is decked in borrowed plumage excites him; it enables him to see her, momentarily, as the great lady herself sumptuously arrayed for his pleasure. Here, in the character who receives a change of clothes in someone else as a virtual change of identity, we have the reverse of the character who tries to alter his identity by changing his clothes. As an acute observer Jonson knew that clothes make the man oftener than we sometimes think; as a lifelong moralist he severely disapproved. Carry the assumptions of Sir Epicure and Nick Stuffe far enough, and they lead to a world of total illusion, in which clothes are the only reality, the world of Swift's digression on clothes in *A Tale of A Tub*, or of *Sartor Resartus* – which is also, needless to add, the world of the theatre.

Wherever we look, then, within the plays or outside them, in structure or in moralizing comment, we find a distrust of theatricality, particularly as it manifests itself in acting, miming, or changing, and a corresponding bias in favour of the 'real' – the undisguised, unacted, and unchanging. This is reinforced by a preference for simplicity as against ornament. One of Jonson's most famous poems begins by eulogizing a country house for its unpretentiousness:

> Thou art not, PENSHURST, built to envious show,
> Of touch, or marble; nor canst boast a row
> Of polish'd pillars, or a roofe of gold:
> Thou hast no lantherne, whereof tales are told;

> *Or stayre, or courts; but stand'st an ancient pile,*
> *And these grudg'd at, art reverenc'd the while.*
> *Thou joy'st in better markes, of soyle, of ayre,*
> *Of wood, of water: therein thou art faire.*
> ['To Penshurst,' ll. 1–8]

Nobility here is conceived as a function of plainness, which expresses the sober virtue of the builder. The prized attributes of the house spring from nature – from the attendant soil, air, wood, and water – rather than from art or artifice. Sir Robert Wroth, in the companion poem, is commended for his indifference to public ceremonials. He cares nothing for sheriffs' dinners or lord mayors' feasts.

> *Nor throng'st (when masquing is) to have a sight*
> *Of the short braverie of the night;*
> *To view the jewells, stuffes, the paines, the wit*
> *There wasted, some not paid for yet!*
> ['To Sir Robert Wroth,' ll. 9–12]

With this disobliging (if witty) reflection on the ostentatiousness of masques, we return to our earlier discussion. The masque proves vulnerable on two related counts – showiness and ephemerality – and the two imply each other. That which is designed for outward show must needs be ephemeral; that which has no solidity to recommend it must have recourse to display. The same considerations obtain here as apply to the merry-go-round of fashion imagined by Volpone, Morose, and Sir Epicure for their doxies: to lavish ingenuity and cost on mere outsides is to commit oneself to the objects of sense, and to slight the more genuine 'subjects' of understanding. But the theatre must always do this, and Jonson, in consequence, deeply distrusts it.

It remains to speculate hastily as to why, despite his persistent and at times vehement antitheatricalism, Jonson was nevertheless able to create so many masterpieces for both the public stage and that of the court. We may recall that the wheel of change conjured up in *Cynthia's Revels* springs from the mind of a character named Phantaste. Phantaste alone of the court nymphs is able to let herself go and dream freely. Jonson the moralist may disapprove her refusal to be 'herself,' but Jonson the dramatist has surreptitiously endowed her with some of the negative capability of his own tribe, the power to imagine herself into a variety of alien shapes. Alongside the well-articulated antitheatricalism, that is, there lurks a less acknowledged but nonetheless potent theatricalism. The fact that Volpone, Morose, and Sir Epicure all think of the garbing of their paramours as 'art' serves to underscore the resemblance between the costumer's trade and the poet's, the craft of the cosmetician and that of the playwright. By placing the sacred term 'art' in the unhallowed mouths of these characters, Jonson acknowledges the bond between himself and them even as he repudiates it. The fact that Sir Epicure plans to dress his wench in a 'wardrobe / Richer than *Natures*' may chiefly convey the extravagance of his sensuality, but it may imply as well that sensual pleasure itself contains an imaginative component which distinguishes it from brute satisfaction of appetite among the brutes, that 'art' can transfigure even the grossest of human activities.

A number of Jonson's most attractive characters possess exceptionally active imaginations, and the power to alchemize other human beings into their own agents – the power to create theatrical illusion. In *Epicene* the power belongs mainly to Truewit and his sly friend Dauphine. In *Bartholomew Fair* it is shared, as a kind of community magic, by all the Smithfield vendors, with their toy shops and gingerbread stalls, their pig tents and ale tables, their games and puppet shows. From a dram of substance they have learned to extract a magnum of illusion. Into all these characters Jonson infuses a heavy current of his own creative energy, which counteracts to some extent the formal disapproval he may think he wishes us to feel. Viewed solely in terms of declared doctrine, we would expect the virtuoso showmanship of Face and Subtle to incur sharp reproof from their creator. In fact we find ourselves inextricably enmeshed in their schemes, and shamefully exhilarated by their triumphs. When, in *Volpone*, the reproof does come, in obedience to a morality imposed from outside, we feel betrayed. It seems likely, in short, that it is precisely the uneasy synthesis between a formal antitheatricalism, which condemns the arts of show and illusion on the one hand, and a subversive hankering after them on the other, that lends to Jonson's comic masterpieces much of their unique high tension and precarious equilibrium.

NOTES

1 *The Jacobean Drama*, 2nd ed. (London 1947), 99–100
2 Cf. *The Alchemist*, Prologue, 1–4, and v.v.162–3
3 Cf. *Epicene*, Prologue, 8–11; *The New Inn*, Prologue, 3–9
4 *Discoveries*, 778–9. All citations to Jonson are to *Ben Jonson*, ed. C.H. Herford and Percy and Evelyn Simpson, 11 vols (Oxford 1925–52), with 'i,' 'j,' 'u,' and 'v' normalized.
5 'Ben Jonson and Jacobean Stagecraft,' in *Jacobean Theatre*, ed. John Russell Brown and Bernard Harris, Stratford-upon-Avon Studies I (London 1960), 51
6 Title-page citations are from W.W. Greg, *A Bibliography of the English Printed Drama to 1700*, I (London 1939), 171, 172, 194, 234. No attempt has been made to reproduce the type-faces of the original (except for capitals), or to indicate line divisions or other title-page peculiarities.
7 *The Malcontent* (London 1604; facs. ed., The Scolar Press, Menston, Yorkshire 1970), Sig. A₂

8 Marston, *Plays*, ed. H. Harvey Wood, II (Edinburgh 1938), 143

9 Stephen Orgel, *The Jonsonian Masque* (Cambridge, Mass. 1966), 150

10 Ibid., 149–50

11 Cf. Thomas M. Greene, 'Ben Jonson and the Centered Self,' *SEL*, x (1970), 325–48

BEN JONSON AND
HUMAN NATURE

G.R. HIBBARD

The world of Jonson's major dramas is a fascinating place, incontrovertibly an intriguing place, but scarcely an attractive place. The urban or metropolitan setting, so rigidly adhered to in them, rules out anything much in the way of references to the beauties of nature. Old Knowell, his son, Master Stephen, and Brainworm have to cross Moorfields, in order to get from Hogsden to the City, where the rest of the action of *Every Man in His Humour* will take place; but even if there were 'daisies pied, and violets blue' on the way, they would not notice them, since Brainworm's activities leave them no time for such diversions. And, though imperial Rome was not without its man-made splendours, it would, I think, be wrong to complain because Jonson gives no indication of them in his two Roman tragedies. Nor was he under any compulsion to remind his audience that Venice was, perhaps, the most beautiful city in Europe. It was not its beauty which led him to choose it as the setting for *Volpone*, but three other considerations which have nothing

55

to do with aesthetics but much to do with irony and relevance: its pre-eminence as a centre of trade, its reputation as a republic strict and impartial in its administra-
tion of justice, and its notoriety as a place of luxury, vice,
and well-organised high-class prostitution.

His depiction of London, however, is another matter.
He had been born there, he had grown up there, and, if
his *Part of the Kings Entertainment in Passing to His
Coronation* can be taken as evidence, he was proud of
being a Londoner, since he quotes his master Camden's
praise of the capital:

*totius Britanniae Epitome, Britannicique Imperij sedes,
Regumque Angliae Camera, tantum inter omneis eminet,
quantum (vt ait ille) inter viburna Cupressus.*
[ll. 30–2][1]

There London sounds a splendid place, fully warranting
the dignity of the Latin and the quotation from Virgil.
But it is not this aspect of London that appears in the
plays. The comedies are full of references to the city –
seven columns of them in the index to the Herford and
Simpson edition of his works – but a run of five of the
entries will serve to give their characteristic flavour: 'The
Counters, Cow lane, Cripplegate, Crooked lane, Cuckold's Haven.'[2] Two gaols, three streets with anything but
imposing or prepossessing names, and a notorious spot
on the Thames, marked by a pole bearing a pair of horns,
leave us in no doubt about the features of his native city
which Jonson thought of as appropriate for a comic action. Or, if these *Sortes Simpsonianae* seem too arbitrary
a manner of deciding the issue, let us look at the description of the Hope Theatre given by the Stage-Keeper near
the end of the Induction to *Bartholomew Fair*:

And though the Fayre *be not kept in the same Region,
that some here, perhaps, would haue it, yet thinke, that*

therein the Author *hath obseru'd a speciall* Decorum, *the place being as durty as* Smithfield, *and as stinking euery whit.*

[Induction, 156–60]

Decorum is, of course, the operative word. Jonson, as *The Sad Shepherd* bears eloquent witness, was not unaware of or unappreciative of the charm of the English countryside. Nor was he unresponsive to good building. His poem 'To Penshurst' tells us all that we need to know on that score. Similarly, he could sing of ideal beauty finding its earthly dwelling in the female form, and give expression to the Platonic view that a graceful shape is the outward manifestation of an inner spiritual excellence. He does it in the superb epode, 'Not to know vice at all, and keepe true state,' which he contributed to Chester's *Love's Martyr* and subsequently reprinted in *The Forrest*. There he writes of

> *A beautie of that cleere, and sparkling light,*
>   *Would make a day of night,*
> *And turne the blackest sorrowes to bright ioyes:*
>   *Whose od'rous breath destroyes*
> *All taste of bitternesse, and makes the ayre*
>   *As sweet, as shee is fayre.*
> *A body so harmoniously compos'd,*
>   *As if* Nature *disclos'd*
> *All her best symmetries in that one feature!*
>   *O, so diuine a creature*
> *Who could be false to?* [ll. 93–103]

But there was no place for a figure such as this, or for sentiments of this nature, in Jonsonian comedy.

The beings who do people the comedies are of another sort altogether. Gross, vulgar, appetitive, often diseased or disfigured, they are presented to us in a manner which leaves us in no doubt about the way in which Jonson intends us to see them. There is a marked stress on their physical appearance. Justice Overdo calls Ursula 'the very *wombe*, and *bedde* of enormitie' (*Bartholomew Fair*, II.ii.106), thus adding the coping-stone to her own evocation of herself as a female Falstaff:

I am all fire, and fat, Nightingale, *I shall e'en melt away to the first woman, a ribbe againe, I am afraid. I doe water the ground in knots, as I goe, like a great Garden-pot, you may follow me by the S.S.ᵉ I make.*

[*Ibid.*, II.ii.50–4]

Ursula is indeed the 'mother o' the Pigs' (II.v.75), as greasy in speech as she is in person, a monstrous sow wallowing in the sty that is Smithfield. Over against her, by way of contrast, let us set the figure of Subtle as he was when Face first met him before the action of *The Alchemist* began. Reminding him of the occasion, Face says:

> But I shall put you in mind, sir, at pie-corner,
> Taking your meale of steeme in, from cookes stalls,
> Where, like the father of hunger, you did walke
> Piteously costiue, with your pinch'd-horne-nose,
> And your complexion, of the romane wash,
> Stuck full of black, and melancholique wormes,
> Like poulder-cornes, shot, at th'artillerie-yard.
> ...
> When you went pinn'd vp, in seuerall rags,
> Yo'had rak'd, and pick'd from dung-hills, before
>   day,
> Your feet in mouldie slippers, for your kibes,
> A felt of rugg, and a thin thredden cloake,
> That scarce would couer your no-buttocks –
>   [*The Alchemist*, I.i.25–37]

The word 'no-buttocks' seems to me to be stamped

with Jonson's seal. He is intensely aware of man's fleshly nature, or, in this particular case, of what might be termed his short-of-flesh-ly nature, and with this there goes his insistence on the natural functions of the body. The processes of excretion have their place in the plays, as well as the activities of eating and drinking. In *Bartholomew Fair* Win Littlewit's need to make water has its effect on the action; and the means by which her husband suggests that need be met — one of Ursula's dripping-pans — makes one realise how deeply engrained the Elizabethan habit of punning was, as well as bringing one face to face with the insanitary horrors of the time. Nor is this all. It is hard to think of any other play in which the dénouement is precipitated by a woman's desperate cry for a basin to spew in. Jonson had used the basin before, at the end of *Poetaster*, but with a difference. There Crispinus merely brings up inkhorn terms, not vomit as Mistress Overdo does. A comparison between the two scenes demonstrates the extent to which allegory can soften the blow, and leaves one wondering whether the men of the Middle Ages did not adopt the allegorical method as a means of reaching some sort of compromise with the otherwise intolerable, rather than as a way of revealing the truth.

Be that as it may, what I am trying to establish is that Jonson insists, as I think no other dramatist of the time does, on those things which man shares with the rest of the animal creation. In his plays we are never allowed to forget for long the dirt, the squalor, and the mess of which human life is so largely made up, 'the fury and the mire of human veins,' as W.B. Yeats puts it. It is true that he can, when the needs of a play demand it, picture the loveliness of the human body also. But when this happens, as it does in the account Mosca gives to Volpone of the beauty of Celia, there are overtones, indicative of the speaker's attitude, which go far towards smirching

that beauty with suggestions of venal sexuality. Mosca
says to his patron:

> *O, sir, the wonder,*
> *The blazing starre of* Italie! *a wench*
> *O' the first yeere! a beautie, ripe, as haruest!*
> *Whose skin is whiter then a swan, all ouer!*
> *Then siluer, snow, or lillies! a soft lip,*
> *Would tempt you to eternitie of kissing!*
> *And flesh, that melteth, in the touch, to bloud!*
> *Bright as your gold! and louely as your gold!*
>   [*Volpone*, I.v.107–14]

One has only to place this passage alongside Tambur-
laine's praise of Zenocrate to see what is happening. The
lines that Marlowe's hero utters are a cry of pure, undi-
luted admiration:

> Zenocrate, *louelier than the loue of* Ioue,
> *Brighter than is the siluer Rhodope,*
> *Fairer than whitest snow on Scythian hils ...*
>   [*1 Tamburlaine*, 283–5][3]

For him Zenocrate's beauty and Zenocrate's chastity are
inseparable. But Mosca's calculated addition of the words
'all ouer' to his description of the whiteness of Celia's
skin is a bit of titillation. Similarly, 'tempt,' applied to
her lip, suggests that she is sensually inclined, while the
reiterated comparison with gold in the last line places
her firmly in the category of things to be acquired and
used, even, perhaps, of things that are passed from man
to man.

But, no matter what Mosca may do to it, Celia at least
has natural beauty. It goes with her goodness. Most of
the characters in Jonson's major plays have either lost
such beauty as they once had, or else have never had any.
The victims of that catalogue of diseases which Volpone
recites with such unction in his disguise as Scoto of

Mantua, they stumble their way across the stage, lame, half-blind, or nearly deaf, coughing and spitting as they go. Moreover, in their attempts to conceal or repair the ravages of time they resort to artificial aids. Tom Otter, grown brave in his cups, and thinking his wife is out of earshot, takes his revenge on the woman who bought him in the marriage market by listing the various devices she has recourse to in order to hide the naked truth:

And she has a perruke, that's like a pound of hempe, made up in shoo-thrids ... A most vile face! and yet shee spends me fortie pounds a yeere in mercury, *and hogs-bones. All her teeth were made i' the* Blacke-Friers: *both her eye-browes i' the* Strand, *and her haire in* Siluer-street. *Euery part o' the towne ownes a peece of her ... She takes her selfe asunder still when she goes to bed, into some twentie boxes; and about next day noone is put together againe, like a great* Germane *clocke: and so comes forth and rings a tedious larum to the whole house, and then is quiet againe for an houre, but for her quarters.*
[*Epicoene*, IV.ii.88–101]

Jonson is still emphasizing man's physical nature; but, while the defects and the decay that time brings to the organism are also found in the animal kingdom, the means taken to combat and conceal them are not. The ingenuity that Mistress Otter exercises and avails her-self of is peculiarly human; and Jonson is fascinated by it. Complaints about women's painting themselves are common enough in Elizabethan drama; but no other playwright of the time devotes so much attention to the matter, has such an intimate knowledge of the processes involved, and makes such deadly use of that knowledge as he does. Much of the total significance of *Sejanus* crystallizes out in that mordant scene, near the beginning of Act II, in which the physician Eudemus gives Livia beauty treatment which also contrives to be Sejanus treatment; for here the physical deception that we see being wrought under our eyes is the first stage in a carefully planned campaign of moral deception. Sejanus pretends to love Livia, in order to secure her connivance and assistance in his design to have her husband Drusus poisoned, so that he may then marry her, thus linking himself to the imperial family and preparing the way for his overthrow of Tiberius. Unfortunately for him, Tiberius Caesar proves to be an even more adroit exponent of the art of deception than he is.

It was with the writing of this play, and in particular, I think, with the writing of this specific scene, that Jonson stepped straight into the dramatic world that we now recognize as being uniquely his. It was here that he really found himself as a playwright and a dramatic poet. Like the hedgehog in that fragment of Archilochus which Isaiah Berlin uses so effectively in his book *The Hedgehog and the Fox*, Jonson, by the time he had finished *Sejanus*, knew 'one big thing.' For the next thirteen years, right down to his completion of *The Devil is an Ass* in 1616, he was to continue exploring the possibilities and the implications of this 'one big thing' in play after play. It lies at the heart of his central achievement as a dramatist. But what exactly is it? Professor L.C. Knights, who was, I think, the first critic to recognise the writing of *Sejanus* as the turning point in Jonson's career, thought, at the time when his *Drama and Society in the Age of Jonson* was published in 1937, that the main concern of *Volpone* and *The Alchemist* was 'the double theme of lust and greed' (p. 207). The Jonson he presented to us there could have said with Chaucer's Pardoner:

> My theme is alwey oon, and ever was –
> 'Radix malorum est Cupiditas.'

It was, as I have good cause to remember, a wonderfully liberating approach. My own interest in Jonson stems directly from my reading of Professor Knights's book when it first came out. The accumulated dust of pedantic learning, which had hidden Jonson from view for so long, was blown away. We heard him speaking to us, in a tone that demanded attention, about things that really mattered. To provide the conditions in which one's author can be listened to once again after years of misunderstanding and neglect is, surely, the highest reward and the greatest satisfaction that the practice of literary criticism has to offer. But the isolation of lust and greed as the main themes of Jonsonian comedy meant that *Epicoene* had to be dismissed as 'pure entertainment' (p. 196). Furthermore, Professor Knights ignored *Bartholomew Fair* completely, though the adventures of Mistress Overdo would seem to indicate that lust was not exactly missing from Jonson's Smithfield, and Busy's consumption of two and a half sucking pigs at one sitting can hardly be cited as an instance of sobriety and moderation. Could it be that Professor Knights's implicit judgment on these two plays was affected by the fact that they are in prose, and do not, therefore, lend themselves to that close concern with the texture of Jonson's verse which is such a splendid feature of his book?

Whatever the truth about this may be, Professor Knights was still of the opinion that in both these plays 'the fun is divorced from any rich significance' (p. 314) when he wrote his essay 'Ben Jonson, Dramatist' for the Penguin volume, *The Age of Shakespeare*, published in 1955. His definition of what the other great plays are about had, however, by this time undergone a striking change. He now wrote of them:

They define with precision a permanent aspect of human nature. For what they isolate for sardonic inspection is a form of folly which, however grotesque in its dramatic

representation, in Sejanus, Mammon, or Meercraft, is not
confined to fools; it is simply the folly of inordinate
desire.[4]

That summation of what Jonson is doing commands far
more assent than the earlier one because it applies to
much more of what we actually see and hear when one
of the plays is performed. Lust and greed do indeed govern the behaviour of the three gulls in *Volpone* up to the
end of the third act. But their actions from that point onwards are not, I think, so easily accounted for solely in
these terms. The two sins also have their obvious bearing
on the behaviour of Volpone himself; but, in his case, they
are not altogether adequate from the outset, and, once
the first trial scene is over, they simply will not do at all.
The itch to torment his victims even further, which gains
a complete hold over Volpone at this stage in the action,
is not a manifestation of lust and greed in any ordinary
sense of those words, but rather of an inveterate malice,
coupled with the desire for a new kind of thrill that only
danger can provide. He is like a powerful car which has
developed such a momentum that it is out of control altogether. Somewhere within Volpone – and it is this, perhaps, which gives the play its extra dimension, making it
different from, and more disturbing than, any other play
that Jonson wrote – there is a consuming drive towards
self-destruction. In that final scene, as he pulls down on
top of himself the monstrous edifice of lies that he has
constructed, rather than yield to Mosca's blackmailing
pressure, he appears like a godless Samson.

'Inordinate desire' comes much closer to defining the
essence of what lies curled up in the hedgehog; but it, too,
has its shortcomings. My dissatisfaction with it springs
largely, I think, from its abstract quality. It does not come
into a sufficiently intimate contact with what seems to me
to be actually going on in the plays; nor does it tie up as

firmly as I should like with that insistence on man's physical nature about which I have said so much already. I want something that refers much more immediately to the senses. And, as must be apparent enough, I should like something that would give *Epicoene* and *Bartholomew Fair* a place within the 'one big thing.' So I go to Jonson himself for a lead. He gives it to me in the last act *The Alchemist*. In the first scene of that act Lovewit, just back from the country, is in animated conversation with his neighbours outside his house. Agog with excitement, the neighbours paint a vivid picture of the frenzied activity that has been going on in and around the house during his absence. Lovewit then asks them whether they have seen anything of Jeremy his butler. They all say no. Much puzzled, Lovewit knocks at the door. There is no answer. He therefore asks one of the neighbours, a blacksmith, to fetch his tools, in order to force an entry. Then, when the man has gone, he knocks again. This time the door opens, and out comes Face, minus the beard he wore in his role as an army captain. He is immediately recognized as the missing Jeremy; and, in answer to Lovewit's query as to why the house is shut up, he replies that he has kept it tight closed for the past month, ever since the cat came in one night with the plague on her. This lie is quite enough to prevent Lovewit from venturing inside; but he is still puzzled to know why his neighbours have had so much to say about visitors going in and out. He therefore turns to Face once more, and this dialogue follows:

LOV. *Breath lesse, and farder off. Why, this is stranger!*
The neighbours tell me all, here, that the dores
Haue still been open — FAC. *How, sir!* LOV. *Gallants, men,*
                    and women,
And of all sorts, tag-rag, beene seene to flock here
In threaues, these ten weeks, as to a second Hogs-den,
In dayes of Pimlico, *and* Eye-bright! FAC. *Sir,*

65

Their wisedomes will not say so! LOV. *To day, they speake*
Of coaches, and gallants; one in a French-hood,
Went in, they tell me: and another was seene
In a veluet gowne, at the windore! diuerse more
Passe in and out! FAC. *They did passe through the dores*
                          then,
Or walls, I assure their eye-sights, and their spectacles;
For here, sir, are the keyes: and here haue beene,
In this my pocket, now, aboue twentie dayes!
And for before, I kept the fort alone, there.
But, that 'tis yet not deepe i'the after-noone,
I should beleeue my neighbours had seene double
Through the black-pot, and made these apparitions!
For, on my faith, to your worship, for these three weekes,
And vpwards, the dore has not beene open'd. LOV.
                          Strange!
NEI. 1. *Good faith, I thinke I saw a coach!* NEI. 2. *And I too,*
I'ld ha' beene sworne! LOV. *Doe you but thinke it now?*
And but one coach? NEI. 4. *We cannot tell, sir:* IEREMIE
Is a very honest fellow. FAC. *Did you see me at all?*
NEI. 1. *No. That we are sure on.* NEI. 2. *I'll be sworne o'*
                          that.
LOV. *Fine rogues, to haue your testimonies built on!*
[Re-enter THIRD NEIGHBOUR, with his tools]
NEI. 3. *Is* IEREMIE *come?* NEI. 1. *O, yes, you may leaue your*
                          tooles,
We were deceiu'd, he sayes. NEI. 2. *He'has had the keyes:*
And the dore has beene shut these three weekes. NEI. 3.
                          Like enough.
LOV. *Peace, and get hence, you changelings.*   [v.ii.15–44]

The worthy neighbours do not know what they have seen,
are no longer sure that they have seen anything at all.
Confronted with the unexpected appearance of Jeremy,
and with his confident assertions, they first doubt, and
then disregard, the evidence of their own eyes. At this

66

point, however, the gulls arrive, demanding the return of
their money and goods; and the neighbours recognize
them as the people they saw going in and out of the
house. Nevertheless, Face still tries to brazen matters out,
telling his master:

> Good faith, sir, I beleeue,
> There's no such thing. 'Tis all deceptio visus. [v.iii.61–2]

In a profound sense, of which Face himself is not fully
aware, he is absolutely right; for deceptions of the vision,
optical illusions, and failures of perception are precisely
what *The Alchemist* is about; and, if one extends the deception to the senses of hearing and touch as well, they
are, I venture to suggest, what Jonson's greatest plays
are about. In the course of the action which is now drawing to its end Lovewit's house has been all things to all
men, a veritable palace of illusions. Dapper has seen it
as the home of the Queen of the Fairies, and he still continues to see it in this light even after his being locked up
in the privy. Drugger has regarded it as the dwelling of a
learned man, a conjurer and master of astrology, who will
provide him with infallible recipes for doing good business. For Ananias and Tribulation Wholesome, it has
been the laboratory of a brilliant scientist, admittedly one
of the wicked, but one who may, nonetheless, become an
instrument 'For the restoring of the silenc'd Saints'
(iii.i.38). To Sir Epicure Mammon it has appeared as
nothing less than the New World itself in all its imagined
richness.

Two kinds of optical illusion have been at work to produce the transmutation, the conversion – both these al-
chemical terms are very relevant – that an ordinary house
in the Blackfriars has undergone in the eyes of these
characters. On the one hand, there is the optical illusion
deliberately contrived by another to mislead the beholder.
It is this that Jonson has in mind in the brief passage in

the *Discoveries* which he devotes to the subject of painting, a passage which shows that he was interested in
theories of vision. He writes, condensing some remarks
by the Jesuit Antonio Possevino in his *Bibliotheca Selecta
Qua agitur De Ratione Studiorum* (Rome 1593):

From the Opticks *it* [Painting] *drew reasons; by which it
considered, how things plac'd at distance, and a farre off,
should appeare lesse: how above, or beneath the head,
should deceive the eye, &c.* [1556–9]

On the other hand, there is the optical illusion which
results from a defect of vision, or – and here the emphasis
moves from physical vision to moral vision – from a deliberate, self-willed refusal to look at the truth, even when
it presents itself in an undeniable form. It is this latter
that Jonson has in mind in what is, so far as I know, the
only previous use of the term *deceptio visus* in his
writings. This occurs in the final scene of *Every Man Out
of His Humour*, when Macilente brings Deliro, the foolish
doting husband of Fallace, to where he sees the spectacle
of his wife being kissed by Fastidious Brisk. Deliro might
well attempt, like Shakespeare's Troilus in a similar
situation, to 'swagger himself out on's eyes' (*Troilus and
Cressida*, v.ii.134), but Macilente gives him no chance to
do so. Rubbing in the truth with an evident delight, the
envious scholar says:

*Why, looke you, sir, I told you, you might haue suspected
this long afore, had you pleas'd; and ha' sau'd this labour
of admiration now, and passion, and such extremities as
this fraile lumpe of flesh is subiect vnto. Nay, why doe
you not dote now, signior? Mee thinkes you should say
it were some enchantment,* deceptio visus, *or so, ha? if
you could perswade your selfe it were a dreame now,
'twere excellent: faith, trie what you can do, signior; it*

68

may be your imagination will be brought to it in time,
there's nothing impossible. [v.xi.6–15]

All the plays, including *Catiline*, that Jonson wrote
between 1603 and 1616 are concerned with deception in
some form or other. The main characters in them fall into
two broad groups: the deceivers and the deceived. The
instrument of deception is the creation of illusions
through the stimulating of the imagination, for which,
as Macilente observes, 'there's nothing impossible'; and
behind the whole process there lies man's infinite capacity for deceiving himself.

The most obvious means of giving others a false impression is the use of disguise. In Shakespearian comedy,
and also in *King Lear*, disguise is normally resorted to as
a means of concealment and protection, though Viola in
Twelfth Night has other ends in view as well, and Portia
in *The Merchant of Venice* is not concerned with self-
protection at all. Her adoption of the role of 'a young
doctor of Rome' comes very close to the purpose for
which disguise is employed in Jonsonian comedy, that of
imposing on others to secure one's own ends. And, with
the assumption of disguise there goes, naturally enough,
play-acting. The two devices, working together, can, on
occasion, produce unexpected and very subtle consequences. In the case of Volpone, there is a sense in which
the disguise he assumes is, for the unclouded vision, not
a concealment of his true nature but a revelation of it. In
the first place, there are strongly marked overtones of
prostitution about the role he takes on and about the
setting in which he places himself. There is no missing
that bed which serves as a focus for the action up to the
end of Act III. One by one, the customers are ushered in
by Mosca, who is very much the bawd, and care is exercised to ensure that they do not encounter one another.

Like women in Iago's diatribe against them, he is one of those who 'rise to play, and go to bed to work' (*Othello*, II.i.115).[5] Moreover, Volpone, like the prostitute, paints his face in order to make himself attractive to his clients. The analogy is clearly right, for he is a prostitute, one who hires out his body for gain. But there is more to it than this. In a manner that fits in perfectly with the topsy-turvy nature of the world Jonson creates, the attraction Volpone exerts depends directly on his repulsiveness. He paints, not to make himself look healthier than he really is, as the normal prostitute does, but in order to make himself look more diseased than he is. The nearer he can come to giving a convincing rendering of a man *in extremis*, the greater is the pull he exerts on the birds of prey who flock about him. Once again, the deception reveals the truth. To the moral vision Volpone is a corpse, the rotting, stinking parody of what man should be. The physical illusion he creates is an emblem of his real nature.

The extra significances that Jonson gives to Volpone's deceptions are, however, things that one only becomes aware of gradually, as a result of reading and re-reading. What is clear from one's first acquaintance with the play is that the diseased, moribund role, which he plays with such zest and vigour, is designed to deceive the eyes of his victims.

With the gulls, we are in the presence of the other kind of optical illusion, the sort that Macilente ironically bids Deliro practise. They see only what they want to see, and deliberately refuse to see what is staring them in the face, because to do so would be too painful, too disillusioning. Admittedly, Volpone gives them every possible assistance; but it is not, in the last analysis, the Fox's acting or Mosca's adroit stage management that takes them in, but their own determination to believe what they wish to believe. There is no need to list the evidence that they are being cheated which piles up before them in the first three acts, as they are systematically milked of gold, jewels, and so forth. Yet they consistently ignore it, because to them the illusion they cherish, that they are about to inherit Volpone's estate, is far more precious than anything else in life. A son's future, a wife's chastity, are as nothing in comparison with it. The shadow has usurped the place of reality. One is reminded of Sejanus's plan to manipulate Tiberius Caesar by showing him

> *the shapes*
> *Of dangers, greater then they are (like late*
> *Or early shadowes) ...*
> *[Sejanus,* II.384–6]

How deep and firm this attachment to illusion is only becomes fully plain after Volpone's attempted rape of Celia. As the court assembles to try the Fox, the Avocatori are unanimous in their acceptance of the account Bonario and Celia have given of what took place. But it is something the gulls cannot take. To do so would mean abandoning the illusive hopes by which they live. Therefore, despite their fears and suspicions of one another, they band together to support the lie that will, they trust, preserve the illusion. And there is no question, even in their warped minds, that the lie is a lie. Mosca reminds them explicitly of precisely what it is that they have to do when they meet at the Scrutineo. He asks them point-blank:

> *Is the lie*
> *Safely conuai'd amongst vs? is that sure?*
> *Knowes euery man his burden?* [IV.iv.3–5)

Volpone is emphatically a play about deception; but those who are deceived in it ask to be deceived, because they deceive themselves. Mosca makes the point for us, in case we may have missed it, when, after the first trial is over, he is reviewing it all with his master. Volpone, in a state of mind where a profound sense of relief is mixed with a growing sense of triumph and elation, can hardly credit his success. He asks Mosca:

> *That, yet, to me's the strangest! how th'hast borne it!*
> *That these (being so diuided 'mongst themselues)*
> *Should not sent some-what, or in me, or thee,*
> *Or doubt their owne side.*

The answer he receives is:

> *True, they will not see't.*
> *Too much light blinds 'hem, I thinke. Each of 'hem*
> *Is so possest, and stuft with his owne hopes,*
> *That any thing, vnto the contrary,*
> *Neuer so true, or neuer so apparent,*
> *Neuer so palpable, they will resist it –* [v.ii.19–27]

The senses, says Mosca, are reliable guides to the truth. What can be seen, and what can be touched, is there; but the message the senses transmit will be blocked on its way to the brain if some illusory hope stands in the way. To be possessed by such hopes is to be possessed by the devil.

But the gulls are not the only self-deceivers. In this very scene Volpone falls into the same error. He also is the victim of an illusion. He has fallen in love with his ability to assume disguises and with the pleasure he derives from vexing others. It is precisely this weakness in him that Mosca plays on when he suggests to the Fox that Voltore, in recompense for his labours on their behalf in court, deserves

> *very richly –*
> *Well – to be cosen'd.* [v.ii.46–7]

Furthermore, Volpone has come to think of himself as invulnerable. It is this ultimate illusion which leads him to have it given out that he is dead. There is a mordant irony at work here.

Jonson's perception of the price that men are willing to pay in order to preserve their illusions governs the structure of *Volpone*, just as it governs the structure of *The Alchemist*. In both plays there is a point at which it seems that the action must come to an abrupt end. In *Volpone* this point is reached at the end of Act III, when Bonario prevents the rape of Celia. In *The Alchemist* it is postponed until IV.vi, the scene in which Surly reveals himself to Subtle and Face, making it clear to them that he now knows exactly what has been going on. Again it looks as though the truth must come out, and again it fails to. Guided and manipulated by Face, the gulls unite to get rid of Surly because he is a threat to their hopes. And, once more, Jonson hammers home the part that self-deception has played in the comedy. In the last scene Lovewit tells Mammon, who is demanding that his money and goods be returned to him:

If you can bring certificate, that you were gull'd of 'hem,
Or any formall writ, out of a court,
That you did cosen your selfe: I will not hold them.

[v.v.68–70]

But, while *The Alchemist* confirms that self-delusion and self-deception are, indeed, the things that Jonson 'isolates for sardonic inspection,' it also tells us even more than *Volpone* does about the way in which illusions can be stimulated until they bloom into gigantic fantasies. The processes used by the alchemists, together with their technical jargon, are part of the play's essential texture. As early as line 19 of the first scene the jargon makes its appearance, when Subtle, after explaining that he found Face a mere serving-man, goes on to say of him that he is now 'by my meanes, translated suburb-Captayne.' One of the central ideas on which the play rests has been

73

introduced – no matter whether other metals can or cannot be transmuted into gold, men can. Face, Subtle, and Doll have, in a special sense, found the philosopher's stone. Face's task is to discover those who cherish dreams of wealth, to learn the specific form these dreams take, and then to lure the gulls to Lovewit's house. There Subtle works on their illusions in the same way that the alchemist worked on base metals. He heats them by applying imaginative stimulus to them, though in the case of Sir Epicure Mammon the imagination is so heated already as hardly to require any further fomentation. The result is that the gull, transported into a fool's paradise and utterly out of touch with reality, readily hands over the tangible wealth that he has, in the vain hope of seeing it 'multiplied.' The insubstantiality of his expectations is perfectly imaged in iv.v, when there is '*A great crack and noise within,*' followed by the entrance of Face, with the news that 'all the *workes* / Are flowne *in fumo*' (iv.v.57–8).

Epicoene, it seems to me, is part of the same vision of things. Indeed, there are respects in which it images that vision with a directness and clarity that no other of the comedies achieves. The idea of deception is present from the beginning of the first scene, where the Boy tells Clerimont about his reception at Lady Haughty's:

The gentlewomen play with me, and throw me o' the bed; and carry me in to my lady; and shee kisses me with her oil'd face; and puts a perruke o' my head; and askes me an' I will weare her gowne ... [i.i.13–17]

From this moment onwards, deception follows deception right up to the most concise *dénouement* that even Jonsonian comedy has to offer – the gesture with which Dauphine '*takes off Epicoenes perruke*' just fifty lines before the last word of the play is spoken. It is a complete surprise to everyone on the stage. Dauphine has deceived friend and foe alike. But, as we all know, it comes as an even greater surprise to the audience. They have been deceived by Ben Jonson, who has kept the secret from them. Is this a mere trick, designed for a highly theatrical effect, or is it part of the play's meaning? I take the latter view of it. By making his audience share in the surprise of the characters on the stage Jonson is underscoring their kinship with those characters. We, as spectators or readers, have had all the evidence before us that the characters in the play have had, including that ambiguous name *Epicoene*. Moreover, if we are readers, we have had the advantage of a warning not given to those characters, since we have read the alternative prologue that Jonson wrote for his comedy. I know this second prologue was composed to refute the charge that *Epicoene* was aimed at specific persons, but the following lines in it seem to carry a wider implication than that:

> *Then, in this play, which we present to night,*
> *And make the object of your eare, and sight,*
> *On forfeit of your selues, thinke nothing true:*
> *Lest so you make the maker to iudge you.* [11. 5–8]

Could it be that '*some persons impertinent exception,*' to which Jonson objected so strongly, included the criticism that he had not played fair by his audience in not letting them into the secret? It is most unlikely that we shall ever know for certain, but I should like to think that such was the case. It is surely no accident that in this prologue, as in the plays, the relationship between sense impressions and the truth is heavily stressed. Jonson was no more averse from judging his audience than he was from judging his characters.

I have not time to deal with the various purposes that deception serves in *Epicoene*, except to point out that some of the deceptions – I am thinking especially of those which Truewit practises on Sir Amorous La-Foole and Sir John Daw – are designed to bring out the truth. What

I do want to emphasize is that the central deception, the planting of Epicoene as a wife on Morose, is only made possible because Morose deceives himself. He marries 'her,' not because he loves her, not even because he desires her, still less for her money, since she has none, but solely to spite and vex his nephew. The long prose soliloquy, which he speaks immediately after he has taken her as his wife, and in which he gloats in imagination over the miseries and indignities that he expects Dauphine to suffer, must be the most extraordinary epithalamion ever written. Obsessed by his hatred of noise and by his passion to put down Dauphine, Morose makes the most elementary mistake that one can make about another human being. If there is a practical moral to be extracted from this play, it is: do make sure before you marry that the person you are marrying is of the sex you think; not to do so is to court frustration and disappointment. His senses, if only Morose would consult them, would tell him the truth. But he makes no use of them. He is wholly out of touch with the basic realities of existence. In other words, he is mad.

It is here, I think, that my unwillingness to accept Professor Knights's isolation of 'inordinate desire' as the main target that Jonson has in view finds its justification. Both words are too limiting. The desires portrayed in the great plays are not merely inordinate, they are, at least in so far as the major characters are concerned, overmastering. They take possession of the entire personality, preventing the proper functioning of both the senses and the reason. Sejanus, Volpone, Sir Epicure Mammon, and, I think, Morose are all in the state that Jonson had recognized and defined when he wrote *Every Man Out of His Humour*, though at that stage in his career he had not yet realized how to present this frame of mind in a wholly dramatic manner. It is the condition described by Asper:

76

As when some one peculiar quality
Doth so possesse a man, that it doth draw
All his affects, his spirits, and his powers,
In their confluctions, all to runne one way ...
[Induction, ll. 105–8]

Even at this early date Jonson, it will be noticed, regards this state of mind as being equivalent to demonic possession, just as he does in *Volpone*. And it is not only desires that can take on this overmastering power; so also can passions and *idées fixes*.

I need this last category, the *idée fixe*, in order to find a place within the total pattern I am proposing for such a figure as that of Adam Overdo in *Bartholomew Fair*. It is Overdo's notion of 'the wise Magistrate,' and the false image he has of himself as 'Iunius Brutus,' that take him to the Fair, disguised as 'mad *Arthur* of *Bradley*' – another example of the disguise that reveals an underlying truth. His illusion that he can see, and see through, knavery leads him to take Edgeworth, the cutpurse, for an innocent young victim of the denizens of the Fair; and his empty dream of the great scene he will stage when he finally exposes the enormities of the place causes him to endure the indignity of being set in the stocks and the other misadventures that come his way. He is in the condition so memorably described by Jonathan Swift in *A Tale of a Tub*:

when a Man's Fancy gets astride *on his Reason, when Imagination is at Cuffs with the Senses, and common Understanding, as well as common Sense, is Kickt out of Doors; the first Proselyte he makes, is Himself ...*[6]

Jonson, I suggest, shared Swift's distrust of the imagination. It is surely significant that he does not, so far as I can recall, use the word at all in that final section of the *Discoveries* which he devotes to the subject of poetry,

77

though it is there, if anywhere, that one might expect to find it; and it can scarcely be an accident that it is precisely the more romantic plays of Shakespeare that elicit his scorn: 'Tales, Tempests, and such like Drolleries' (Bartholomew Fair, Induction, 130) and 'some mouldy tale, / Like Pericles' ('Ode to Himself,' ll. 21–2). It was not, quite obviously, that he was without imagination. The plays he wrote are ample proof of the contrary. But, in so far as Jonson the dramatist is concerned, that imagination only seems to have worked at white heat when he was dealing with the follies, the vices, and the crimes of which man is capable. Whenever he seeks to give a positive representation in a play of the ethical values by which he set such store, something seems to go wrong. Cicero, in Catiline, is clearly meant to embody these values. Orator, moral philosopher, and statesman, he has Jonson's unqualified approval. It is his undoing. He is allowed to commit dramatic suicide by talking himself, the play, and the audience to death. Similarly, when Jonson tries to show sensual attraction between a man and a woman developing – admittedly, with much encouragement from the man's friend – into deep and disinterested friendship, as he does in The Devil is an Ass, he cannot make it convincing. Worse still, the intrusion of this motive into the world he has so successfully created in the rest of the play breaks down the coherence of the whole thing. When Manly, in the climactic scene, urges Wittipoll to practise virtue, instead of taking advantage of Mistress Fitzdottrel's plight, what he says sounds dreadfully abstract and empty, especially when it is set alongside the lively business patter of Meercraft, so full of references to solid, tangible things:

> O friend! forsake not
> The braue occasion, vertue offers you,
> To keepe you innocent: I haue fear'd for both;

78

> *And watch'd you, to preuent the ill I fear'd.*
> *But, since the weaker side hath so assur'd mee,*
> *Let not the stronger fall by his owne vice,*
> *Or be the lesse a friend, 'cause vertue needs him.*
> [IV.vi.28–34]

Morally it is admirable, no doubt, but dramatically it does not work.

Jonson can, of course, find expression in verse for the values he believed in, but not within the framework of a play. To see him doing this kind of thing supremely well, we must turn to his non-dramatic poetry. Earlier in this paper I quoted some lines from his epode 'Not to know vice at all, and keepe true state,' in order to show the response he could make to beauty in woman. I now want to end by quoting the beginning of the same poem, because that, taken in conjunction with the lines about beauty, makes my main point for me.

> *Not to know vice at all, and keepe true state,*
> *   Is vertue, and not Fate:*
> *Next, to that vertue, is to know vice well,*
> *   And her blacke spight expell.*
> *Which to effect (since no brest is so sure,*
> *   Or safe, but shee'll procure*
> *Some way of entrance) we must plant a guard*
> *   Of thoughts to watch, and ward*
> *At th'eye and eare (the ports vnto the minde)*
> *   That no strange, or vnkinde*
> *Obiect arriue there, but the heart (our spie)*
> *   Giue knowledge instantly,*
> *To wakefull reason, our affections king:*
> *   Who (in th'examining)*
> *Will quickly taste the treason, and commit*
> *   Close, the close cause of it.*
> *'Tis the securest policie we haue,*
> *   To make our sense our slaue.*

But this true course is not embrac'd by many:
  By many? scarse by any.
For either our affections doe rebell,
  Or else the sentinell
(That should ring larum to the heart) doth sleepe,
  Or some great thought doth keepe
Backe the intelligence, and falsely sweares,
  Th'are base, and idle feares
Whereof the loyall conscience so complaines.
  Thus, by these subtle traines,
Doe severall passions [still] inuade the minde,
  And strike our reason blinde. [11. 1–30]

The 'one big thing' that Jonson knew is, I conclude, the simple yet massive view of human psychology which those lines condense so admirably and concisely. Here we have Professor Knights's 'inordinate desire' in the shape of those rebellious 'affections'; my 'idées fixes' in the form of that 'great thought' which keeps back the information, brought by the senses, from reaching the reason to which those senses are no longer subject; and, as a consequence, the invasion of the mind by the passions, leading to a blinding of the mental faculties. It is no wonder that the major figures of Jonson's greatest plays are mad.

Yet having said this, I have not, I think, reached the heart of the matter. These lines occur in a poem where the many are contrasted with the few, so few that they are 'scarse ... any.' The poem celebrates the great Platonic triad of Goodness, Truth, and Beauty, coming together in the union of perfect Love. It is this which is known to and treasured by the few. The plays – the great plays – are, of course, about the many, who abandon the realities of Goodness, Truth, and Beauty for their shadowy, insubstantial opposites which, nevertheless, play such a dominant part in the world that we know. Jonson the dramatist exposes these shadows for what they are – illusions. Deep within the realistic hedgehog, the tireless, shrewd, sardonic observer of life, there lay a pearl, the pearl of Platonic idealism; and I don't think he ever lost it.

NOTES

1 The text used for all quotations from Jonson's works, and for all references to them, is that printed in *Ben Jonson*, ed. C.H. Herford and Percy and Evelyn Simpson (Oxford 1925–52).

2 XI.647

3 *The Works of Christopher Marlowe*, ed. C.F. Tucker Brooke (Oxford 1910)

4 *The Age of Shakespeare*, ed. Boris Ford (Harmondsworth 1955), 316

5 Quotations from Shakespeare are taken from *William Shakespeare: The Complete Works*, ed. Peter Alexander (London & Glasgow 1951)

6 Jonathan Swift, *A Tale of a Tub*, ed. A.C. Guthkelch and D. Nichol Smith (Oxford 1920), 171

'THE STAPLE OF NEWS'
AND THE LATE PLAYS

One of the most rewarding, and worrying, things about
Jonson is his accessibility to criticism. It is not that his
works are so richly varied that they become an

> *Ocean where each kind*
> *Does streight its own resemblance find ...*

giving the Critic as Narcissus a ready but watery reflection of himself. They are too firmly defined for that. Nor
do I mean to suggest that they do not demand an analyti-
cal brilliance and fine sensibility to social conduct if
Jonson's skills and the ethical concerns which they serve
are to be realised with any truth. Indeed the erudition of
his recent editors and interpreters, the

> *Schollers, that can iudge and fair report*
> *The sense they heare, aboue the vulgar sort,*
> [*The Staple of News*, Prologue for the Court]

is exemplary in the best Jonsonian manner. The remark
by John Addington Symonds that Jonson 'put nothing

into his plays which patient criticism may not extract'
underestimates their subtlety of organisation as well as
the problems of articulating their leading ideas in critical
terms which test our own understanding of what society
is and should be. And yet they *are* amenable to analysis
and commentary which in a demonstrable and comprehensive way are capable of telling the truth about them,
almost as if the criticism were a controlled projection
from them. Because each play is itself a form of investi-
gation, with its central idea and ingeniously elaborated
structure, we sense immediately both the possibilities
of and the real contribution offered in papers on the
'theme' or 'structure' of *Volpone*, *The Alchemist*, *Bartholomew Fair*. Art's hid causes *may* be found. Beyond
that, there is clearly a sense in which Jonson criticism
is cumulative and coherent, reflecting the works themselves, for each play adds to the œuvre, diversifying
it but also advancing it; and when in a late play like
The Magnetic Lady, 'finding himselfe now neare the
close or shutting up of his Circle', Jonson makes
explicit both the continuities within his work and his
pursuit of total form, we at once acknowledge this artistic
and intellectual integrity. We may go even further, citing
the poems as a complementary corpus positively affirming
a civilised order subverted in the plays and harmoniously
re-formed in the masques, so that taken together and
cemented by the *Discoveries*, they embody the man himself in a way which transcends only in its extended unity
the monumentally self-defining *Workes of Beniamin
Jonson*. This idea of the man engaged in, indeed embodied
by, the works, far from complicating their assessment by
diluting criticism with psychology, has led to a fruitful
branching of inquiry. The metamorphoses of the satirist
figure, his gradual incorporation in the action, the dis-
persal of his functions through several characters, the
tempering of judgment, serve our understanding of

84

Jonson's personal development while imbuing the criticism with a self-endorsing moral seriousness. The relation of the poet to his society, his creations, and his customers, about which Jonson is so explicit, at one end of the scale opens out onto the real world of economic, religious, political, and social abuses and at the other brings them home to an actual flesh and blood audience whose immediate physical response in pleasured recognition, bemused stupidity, or aggressive rejection Jonson has somehow already made part of the drama. Even this compression of the spectrum, instead of confounding the categories, seems merely to yield a deeper truth — that history *is* aesthetics or, conversely and more conventionally, that criticism inevitably leads out towards history. But either way it is an enrichment of the possibilities for criticism. In between, while the characters beat out the forms of their creations in imaginative pursuit of some gilded nature or perfected justice, it is impossible to resist the analogies with Jonson's own role as dramatic artificer, so that affirming Jonson's craft of theatre is one with analysis of his characters' ingenuity in play-making, whether it is conceiving and directing an intrigue, enticing an audience, acting in disguise, setting a scene, finding a theatre, creating multiple perspectives on the action, distracting the eyes with gold, the nostrils with roast pig, the ears with ballads, or the mind with rhetoric. This deployment of the arts of theatre in an almost critically distanced way makes his plays a valuable source of identifiably theatrical forms. Since these further exemplify a sophisticated marriage of elements of old comedy, new comedy, native moralities, and popular 'shews,' each form demands its own scholarship; their structures, by relation to the past, assume a mythic depth or parodic surface; their integration frames Jonson's original response to change and signals his larger effort to inform the new order with values derived from the past adapted

85

to the present. This same principle is at work in his translations and in the rich allusiveness of his poetry. Similarly, the linguistic variety of his plays, like their multiple plotting, offers the characteristic blend of local vigour and decorous relationship which makes commentary on it such a happy mixture of the particular and the general.

By now you will have discerned in this Jonsonian induction a familiar note of unease surfacing beside the slightly too insistent affirmations. You may even think that this attempt to say something about *The Staple of News* is perilously close to Jonson's later position of making, not plays, but models of plays. So let me be explicit.

My way into a judgment of the late plays, including *The Devil is an Ass*, is to see them simply as a reaction to the popular success of the middle comedies. They are a final attempt to come to terms with the problem of audience implication and to insist on the primacy of his judgment over theirs. The satirist's and teacher's dilemma, the impossibility of bringing to knowledge those too obtuse to see their folly, prompts Jonson to develop an impressive dramatic strategy for showing them – literally – what fools they are. But precisely because this formidable technique is so skilfully directed to taking in, framing, ridiculing, and then expelling his intractable audience, the plays themselves become inclusive, self-sufficient, and self-validating worlds. Endlessly and satisfyingly intricate in their internal relations, refined and deepened by selective use of the past and by plausible correspondences with the present, they create in turn a metaworld of criticism and scholarship whose terms of reference and content have been virtually predetermined by Jonson's forbiddingly intellectual effort of containment. Disengagement from their complete worlds, without being brutally destructive or broadly dismissive, is almost impossible. Jonson clings to his art in these plays, and so long as he stays within their magic circle his insights and the dependent criticism which notes them have an admirable density and cogency. But like Volpone, the moment he leaves his art-world and its controls to glory in the street, confusing the distinctive realities of art and nature, he loses his authority and falls prey to the real world. Whether it is a closed garden, a Bosch globe, or even a yellow submarine, the shutting up of the circle is not only an act of containment but an act of exclusion.

It is this exclusiveness of the later plays that worries me. It is not adequately explained as an 'artistic decline' or a failure to realise his designs in fully dramatic terms. The social conscience is as alert as ever, the fighting spirit as strong, the values he seeks to communicate are timeless, the literary traditions he draws on and works within, including parody of their degenerate forms, are indisputably the most fruitful way of defining and experiencing what we mean by civilisation, his innovative skill is everywhere evident. It is just that nobody any longer listens, because he himself has no ears for what we too are fraternally bound to call the new illiteracy. There are compelling analogies with critics and criticism in our own time, faced with the established press and its underground counterpart, with poster-theatre, and even with a political pornography that seems to make any civilised debate which is also fully democratic an impossible ideal. Jonson blames his audience for their failure to understand, but more significant than any self-exculpating pique is the prior distrust of their independent judgment which his dramatic structuring reveals. After *Bartholomew Fair* the reformation of society proceeds too literally by the purgation, segregation, or expulsion of its jeerers.

It is commonly agreed that Jonson was most at ease with his audience in *Bartholomew Fair*. His 'pretty gradation' from the everyday world to the theatre, the contract which binds audience and players in a common enterprise, the analogous entry of the visitors as audience to the fair with its company of stall-holders, their union in turn as a combined audience to the puppets, and even the invitation to supper, have one thing in common – a shared perspective. Everyone is looking the same way. The only difference is that the theatre audience sees most and therefore contains them all. There are of course many inner analogies, one of the finest of which is the purse-cutting scene, where the poetic text ('*Relent and repent, and amend and be sound*'), the moral stance and criminal act, have their own graduated scale of stage observers, from the absorbed Cokes to the all-seeing Quarlous and Winwife. But the puppets on whom this unified world of men and players fix their attention are also both an expression and a resolution of Jonson's own equivocal attitude to theatre. They confute Busy, and so even at its most vulgar and dehumanized, theatre has a function in transforming the images of wickedness with which men stock their minds. Like the mechanicals' play in *A Midsummer Night's Dream*, the puppet show reduces drama to its most fundamental form for the most simple-minded audience, and it works superbly. However sophisticated the frame and ironically allusive the myth, it is as primitive as street-theatre and shows a similar paradox in the insecure command of its own fantasies, for its actors naively move from play world to real world with a disturbing insouciance. The coarse and the fine, the verbal and visual, are one, and although there is no sentimental indulgence of folly and the admonition to go mend still stands, there is here a generous acknowledgment of the audience's basic humanity. It is a happy point of equilibrium which it took Jonson years to reach and which he was soon to lose.

If one thinks for a moment of the artist's predicament –

where *do* I go from here? – and the difficulty of sur-
passing such a coherent play as *Batholomew Fair*, Jonson's conscious ingenuity in shaping a new drama with
The Devil is an Ass must command our respect. Audience
and players were one in watching the puppets, yet what
did the puppets look out on but a mingled world of men
and players in which the only distinguishing mark was
the edge of the stage.

> *They haue their* Vices, *there, most like to* Vertues;
> *You cannot know 'hem, apart, by any difference:*
> *They weare the same clothes, eate o' the same meate ...*
> [*The Devil is an Ass*, i.i.121–3]

In *The Devil is an Ass* Jonson advances his stagecraft
by turning the tables. He puts the old play-characters
on the outside as observers of, or audience to, the natural
human characters of the inner play. More specifically the
world of dramatic art is now represented not by literal
puppets but by the old morality stagers, Satan, Iniquity,
and Pug, who, like pensioners at a matinée, come out of
retirement to look at a new play in which a bunch of
citizen-actors become independent of the poet, quit their
seats, usurp the stage, parade their clothes and their
rhetoric, and hatch hyper-diabolical intrigues. Their
theatrical amateurism is one with their criminal skill or
inherent folly, for they act viciousness and stupidity best
in being themselves. Where in *Bartholomew Fair* all
spoke prose except the puppets and songsters, the men
and women, as becomes their role of players, now assume the artfully natural speech rhythms of the actors'
verse along with their voices, leaving a superannuated
Satan and Iniquity to swap the fourteeners of their hey-
day. Of course Jonson is saying that the devil is an ass,
beaten at his own game by the ordinary people of this
new age and rightly displaced by them; and of course this
amounts to a manifesto claiming that the old theatre has

been outstripped by life and that his own play is, and promotes, a new morality.

Fitzdottrell, however, is the only one who explicitly enacts the movement from audience to stage and thereby projects theatrically the audience's folly. His cloak, described as a stage garment, is probably a traditional Vice-costume. But folly is an epidemical disease, and his is a representative act which Jonson, by projecting and containing, theoretically distances and controls. For Fitzdottrell takes his world with him, a mirror image of the everyday, framed by the old morality. As those will who live in such a world, he makes plays, and in scenes like those between Wittipol and Mrs Fitzdottrell he re-enacts his role of audience breaking in upon the action to play the fool. The play which could not have succeeded in privately shaming his folly now publicly exposes it. The prologue expresses concern that public possession of the stage may make the actors impotent:

> Yet, Grandee's, would you were not come to grace
> Our matter, with allowing vs no place,
>   ... This tract
> Will ne'er admit our vice, because of yours ...
> We know not how to affect you.

Despite this confession of inadequacy, it is Jonson's greater achievement to prove the superiority of his art to circumstance; and the fertility and vigour of Meercraft, together with the intrigues of Wittipol and Manly, make it a lively new play. But the involuted cleverness is already an expression of his final solution. Like Saturn, he begets children only to swallow them. For the organic unity of *Bartholomew Fair*, which also expresses a fully communal spirit, he now offers a structure which is intellectually ingenious and theatrically vivid but also divisive. The projection and ridicule of his intrusive audience, though brilliantly comprehended by the play, even to the point where they make it, mark the beginning of Jonson's movement into an art-world in which he can contain their independence, which he sees only as folly, and be entirely their master. The ending of the play may seem indulgent:

> It is not manly to take ioy, or pride
> In humane errours (we doe all ill things ...)

But its application is sadly limited, for most are barren and only

> The few that haue the seeds
> Of goodness left, will sooner make their way
> To a true life, by shame, then punishment.
> [The Devil is an Ass, v.vii.169–74]

Jonson creates an audience most literally in The Staple of News. The Prologue gets out six words – 'For your owne sake, not ours' – before Gossip Mirth, the spirit of Comedy, who thinks it great fun, clambers on to the stage where she can see and be seen, interrupting the Prologue and hardening Tattle's confidence with the advice: 'be not asham'd.' Set above the groundlings, that audience of 'graue' wits who are not so much serious as dead, they call for stools and sit upon the play. Judgment is physical, like the illumination. The tire-men mend their lights, and with a principled demand for originality and a report on the poet, dead drunk behind the scenes, silent in sack, his book torn, looking like a miserable emblem of patience (in fact, the melancholic artist reduced to inactivity or self-destruction from frustrated idealism), the hard labour ends and the man-midwife-Prologue delivers the play.

It is a vigorous opening which gives all the weight of exasperation to the Prologue's words when at last he is allowed to speak:

For your owne sakes, not his, he bad me say
Would you were come to heare, not see a Play.

One has to be careful in commenting on *The Staple of News* because Mirth has forestalled most critics. She is the dramatic theorist, literary historian, and sharp reviewer, one of a panel of speakers who pointed out long before Dryden that Jonson was a 'decay'd wit.' Expectation understands well enough that it is a prodigal play, and that a literal fool is unnecessary because they are all fools. They know their Jonson, recalling with affection Zeale-of-the-land Busy, keeping an eye out for the mad justice, and proving that they had taken the point of *The Devil is an Ass*, namely that Fitzdottrell was the devil and foolish enough to risk cuckoldry. Mirth extends the idea to the new play, identifying the Vices, although *'now they are attir'd like men and women o' the time.'* She not only calls Peni-boy Senior Old Covetousness but, like Canter, notes the link between money and sex by calling him Money-Bawd and Flesh-Bawd. Peni-Boy Junior of course she rightly calls Prodigality, and Pecunia, *'prank't vp like a prime Lady,'* is Mistress Money. She knows that the play is an allegory to be taken generally and refuses to allow any specific identifications. 'But the play is also a morality play on the value of money,' writes one of Jonson's finest critics.[1] What more do Pecunia's three names do, *'but express the property of Money, which is the daughter of earth, and drawne out of the Mines?'*, asks Mirth, giving the symbolism a bit more resonance. Having identified Peni-boy Junior and praised his lack of jealousy, she then shows her Aristotelian awareness that the Prodigal is more likely than the Miser to become 'communicative,' 'liberall,' and even 'magnificent'; but she also recognises that both urbanity and humanity would appear in the Miser *'an' hee were rightly distill'd.'* There is clearly a trained intelligence behind these comments and it is equally clear from her image of Jonson drunk backstage on royal sherry (the *'most miserable* Embleme *of patience'*) that she is well acquainted with the emblem-books. She has a fashion-ably sharp eye for poet-presenters and sees that Peni-boy Canter is *'a kin to the* Poet.' Her capacity for dis-cerning linguistic links and dramatic enactment shows not only in a readiness to see ironic point in the fact that Smug, who caught a dose of the staggers, was required by his part to be drunk, but in her hope that Jonson's play, although barrelled up so long, might prove true *'to the time of yeer, in* Lent,' and be *'delicate* Almond *butter,'* with its rich suggestion of a winter flowering. Her wit shows to comparable advantage when she antici-pates, but puts more succinctly, Herford and Simpson's point, much repeated since their day, that Jonson's Staple, built upon money greed and 'held together by the cash nexus ... collapses upon the failure of funds.'[2] For when Expectation complains that the poet has let fall the Staple *'most abruptly,'* Mirth quickly adds 'Bankruptly, *indeede!'* This comment by Mirth, original with her, once more converts criticism to paraphrase. If, as many have claimed, the Staple itself is too fleetingly shown, it was Expectation who first said so, criticising both the delay in opening it and its premature end. She was also quick to note in the consequential collapse of the Academy the loss of a new power in popular education and in particu-lar the dashed hopes *'of so many towardly young spirits.'* Or if Peni-boy Canter is too much of a direct moralizer and too little of a human being, Mirth and Tattle at least saw through his sham beggary and wished for a 'Court-Beggar *in good clothes,'* or *'a* begging scholar *in blacke, or one of these beggerly* Poets,' or *'a thred-bare* Doctor of Physicke, *a poore* Quacksaluer,' or *'a* Sea-captaine, *halfe steru'd.'* These may be stereotypes but they meet late morality decorum. More important, they imply

Jonson's failure to offer socially relevant comment on the genuine problem of enforced poverty.

These play-goers were also alert, like Jonson himself, to the seductive arts of theatre. Mistress Trouble Truth recoiled from *The Devil is an Ass*, believing that it taught wives how to cuckold their husbands; her frigid fears command no respect, but Mirth speaks of the risk with a hint of that richness of experience which informs the best criticism. She adds to her misgivings about theatre by pointing out, correctly, that the news offered in the play is '*monstrous! scuruy! and too exotick! ill cook'd! and ill dish'd!*' Logically and responsibly she acts on her distrust and suggests that drama in schools should not be permitted to turn scholars into play-boys, or, to put it another way confirmed in the event, that *The Staple of News* is not really worth studying.

Jonson's projection of his audience of learned owls, wide-eyed but blind, is clearly not just a matter of having a bunch of women of fashion climb on to a stage to give their opinions. It is also a remarkably accurate forecast of subsequent interpretive comment and critical judgment, and a brilliant physical enactment of his deeper point that such intrusion need not be physical at all. There are more ways than one of getting between a play and its author.

> *marke but his wayes,*
> *What flight he makes, how new; And then he sayes,*
> *If that not like you, that he sends tonight,*
> *'Tis you haue left to iudge, not hee to write.*
> [*The Staple of News*, Prologue for the Stage]

The play itself is properly larger than the Staple, for it is Jonson's own Staple of news. It is not synonymous with the city news office but is offered in serious public competition with it. Just as the gossips are part of our Jonson's play, so is the vice of interpretation part of its subject; and if such a literate audience is incapable of truly judging Jonson's carefully structured news, what hope has it, without the poet's help, of judging mere news, made like the time's news?

The play was long preparing, as we know from Jonson's use of similar material in *News from the New World* (1620), *Neptune's Triumph* (1624), and references to Butter, the Infanta, the coronation, and the destruction of some 'parcels of a Play' in his fire of 1623. It is not a sudden reversion after a decade of courtly distractions, but a deeply considered and carefully wrought statement, the comprehensive subject of which determines its fully public form. Its newness is that of a truth about the developing political and social pattern of England; and that sense of where the nation is going *is* more important than Charles, the Infanta or the news office. But Jonson is anxious to demonstrate how his new ways adapt the drama itself to new needs and thereby to show its continuing superiority as a medium of informed public comment.

The on-stage audience now makes literal and refines the analogies of *The Devil is an Ass.* It is part of a larger strategy of theatrical exposure in which appearance is a primary element. Unlike poets, although Jonson does so, actors must provide for their guests 'in the way of showes.' Hence it is a visionary theatre in which the traditional and easily recognised forms are preserved and adapted to the times. The play opens with a sit-in, moves on to costume scenes for young heirs, city liverymen, and academics, and later gives splendid opportunities for spectacle with Pecunia discovered in state, successive assemblies, the feast in Apollo, music and dancing, the beating up of Peni-boy Senior, a beggar unmasked, and the circus act of a mad justice and his performing dogs. It may seem to some that too often 'Jonson relies solely on symbolic action'[8] but this is a concomitant of his concern to thrust the audience into prominence, giving them drama apparently on their own terms, and focussing on their response. That their terms are not wholly his is obvious, which is only to say, as Jonson himself does in his figure of Expectation, that preconceptions are critically disabling and our judgment, unlike his, misguided.

Satan, Iniquity, and Pug disappear altogether and the Fitzdottrells, hardened into morality types, now sit as intrusive, prose-speaking spectators to yet another realistic play within, for it starts with a quite natural scene of Peni-boy Junior putting on his new clothes. With the poet silent and his book torn, this audience has to make its own play, but Mirth soon sees that Peni-boy Junior's situation and costume cast him in the old role of Prodigal; hence the play they are watching must be a morality. In fact, however, within the naturalistic family circle of the Peni-boys, it is Canter who sees the potential of drama in real life and puts the tradition to work in the old style by creating the play of the prodigal son. He, not Jonson, is also its enthusiastic presenter, another who forestalls the critics:

> *See!*
> *The difference 'twixt the couetous, and the prodigall.*
> *'The Couetous man neuer has money! and*
> *'The Prodigall will haue none shortly!*
> [*The Staple of News*, I.iii.38–41]
> *Why, here's the* Prodigall *prostitutes his* Mistresse!
> [*Ibid.*, IV.ii.123]

But this inner world of ordinary people turned morality characters becomes audience to, indeed is dependently wedded to, another inner show, the Pecunia set, a group of figures, less realistic, more symbolic, whose life therefore is not innate but, being allegorical, exists only in our right perception and use of them, as of the drama itself. The morality characters and emblematical figures

now combine as a further audience to see the real everyday world of London life, the Staple of News. But even
this proves to be yet another construction, begotten and
fairly helped into the world by Cymbal.

> *You must be a Mid-wife Sir!*
> *Or els the sonne of a Mid-wife!*
> [*The Staple of News*, i.v.77–8]

In the range of its fictive characters and reported events,
even in its further perspectives of outer and inner rooms,
the Staple is a competing image of the theatre. In its
linguistic variety it meets decorum by matching the style
to the customers and their needs; for the unities of time,
place, and action it has an efficient filing system and an
extensive network which ensures the receipt and co-
ordination of news from all four cardinal quarters of
London – Court, Church, City, and Parliament – and
with Tom the barber on its staff it can even cope with the
arts. True to form, its leading actors 'sustaine their parts'
in cloak and '*Staple* gowne,' Picklock, like Mosca, de-
claring himself

> *A true* Chamaelion, *I can colour for't.*
> *I moue vpon my axell, like a turne-pike,*
> *Fit my face to the parties, and become,*
> *Streight, one of them.*
> [*The Staple of News*, ii.i.35–9]

So this play, in which '*Wit* had married *Order*,' proves
to be another morality and Peni-boy Junior, blinded by
the expertise, plays Gossip to Cymbal's Staple of News.
But this is far from being the innermost play of Jonson's
calculatedly complex nest of successive audience-actor
creations. Indeed, as if on some inflationary spiral, we
go up the dramatic scale as we move towards its centre –
from popular morality to court masque. It is now Peni-
boy Junior's turn to move in on the act. The office is

closed for lunch, and when we meet the group again they have been eating in the Apollo where, fittingly, they make a masque. It begins with an antimasque of jeering,

> *A very wholesome exercise, and comely.*
> *Like lepers, shewing one another their scabs,*
> *Or flies feeding on vlcers.*
> [*The Staple of News*, iv.i.34–6]

But the real creator in this consumer society is Lickfinger. When he re-enters with the ladies the tone rises at once and we re-enact much of another banqueting-hall masque, *Neptune's Triumph*, which was also the cook's work. Lickfinger, who 'has *Nature* in a pot,' can cook, carve and colour it to a perfection which needs no mending by any toothpick art. It is his wisdom, more palatable than Madrigal's, which leads to Peni-boy Junior's fruitfully witty praise of Pecunia as the light of the world. His eulogy is chorused by the others when, as Jonson's note says, '*They all beginne the encomium of* Pecunia,' and this festive conjunction of minds transforms them into a community of kissing cousins. Madrigal, in perfect laureate verse, makes a poem in Pecunia's honour:

> *The splendour of the wealthiest* Mines!
> *The stamp and strength of all imperiall lines,*
> *Both maiesty and beauty shines,*
> *In her sweet face!*

To this he adds words for a saraband, a slow Spanish dance befitting a projected marriage:

> *According to* Pecunia's Grace
> *The Bride hath beauty, blood, and place,*
> *The Bridegroome vertue, valour, wit,*
> *And wisdome, as he stands for it.*

The musicians arrive in Apollo too. The forceful precedent of *Epicoene* is invoked, as it is later confirmed in

THE STAPLE OF NEWS, LATE PLAYS

The New Inn, when words combine with music in the singing of Madrigal's poem. Harmony reigns. The audience is properly spellbound, for Jonson says, '*They are all Struck with admiration.*' The revels begin and everyone dances except Peni-boy Canter, who has now lost control of *his* little play, and like a disaffected Jaques stands audience to the action, waving his finger and offering his own uncomprehending, puritanically dismissive commentary:

> *Look, look, how all their eyes*
> *Dance i' their heads (obserue) scatter'd with lust!*
> *At sight o' their braue* Idoll! *how they are tickl'd,*
> *With a light ayre! the bawdy* Saraband!
> *They are a kinde of dancing engines all!*
> *And set, by nature, thus, to runne alone*
> *To euery sound! All things within, without 'hem,*
> *Moue, but their braine, and that stands still! mere*
>   *monsters,*
> *Here, in a chamber, of most subtill feet!*
> *And make their legs in tune, passing the streetes!*
> *These are the gallant spirits o' the age!*
> *The miracles o' the time! that can cry vp*
> *And downe mens wits! and set what rate on things*
> *Their half-brain'd fancies please!*
>   [*The Staple of News*, IV.ii.130–43]

Like a good monarch, Peni-boy Junior praises his poet and offers him, as monarchs still do, sack and claret for his service. As in *Neptune's Triumph*, however, there is now a second antimasque, which is ushered in by Peni-boy Senior. Like Guyon in the Bower of Bliss he dashes the proferred cup, but he is more than matched by the virtuous Pecunia, who, once dull and tarnished from lack of air, now celebrates her release from this malicious jailor who had kept her a 'close prisoner vnder twenty bolts.' He would have smothered her in a chest and strangled her in leather; but sunlight and air, the liquidity of the dance, here imaged in the masque, have restored her health. The antimasque ends with an excellent comedy of affliction in which the assembly spurns him and kicks him out while the fiddlers drown his noise in music.

Nor is this the innermost play, for 'Spirits are not finely touched but to fine issues.' Prince Peni-boy now applies his new knowledge and prompted by dramatic example enters upon his own creation, one that will serve the professions, knowledge, and society — the College of Canters. The coinage of his brain, a university, lies at the heart of this world made by the audience and players and completes its visionary order. At this point audience, gossips, and actors view the central allegory in a perspective as formally unified as that in *Bartholomew Fair*; and it is precisely at this point, following an immensely colourful, vibrantly alive, and verbally witty masque, when spirits are riding high and a new vision is about to be realised, that Peni-boy Canter plays Buzy to the puppets. Like an unruly and destructive audience he breaks in upon these actors and ensures that their play is still-born. '*It was spitefully done o' the* Poet,' says Censure, '*to make the Chuffe take him off in his heighth, when he was going to doe all his braue deedes!*' Act IV is a tour de force of dramatic construction and ironic overlay and is integrally related to everything that has gone before. The characters, closer to the several arts of theatre than they are to real life, talk and act in accordance with their own understanding of dramatic norms, from the outer morality to the inner masque, each of which has its successive presenters. It is on these planes and in contrivedly theatrical terms that the degenerative actions are played out.

At the end of Act IV *The Staple of News* begins to unwind. The masque is ended, Peni-boy Canter's abduction of Pecunia deprives the Staple-play of its life-force, the gossips (although reluctant to leave) have abused and rejected the poet in their 'mourniuall *of* protests,' and Canter's morality play, which has done its job but is not adequate to a new threat, is superseded.

In a scene which re-enacts the opening of the prodigal play, Peni-boy Junior appears in Canter's patched cloak; but it is also called a *'graue Robe'* and with it he assumes his father's role as redeeming poet and playmaker. At first, like the poet in the tiring house, he is sunk in lethargy, and being rejected thinks he has the *'epidemicall disease'* upon him, but the collapse of the poet's competitor, the Staple of News, arouses him. The last main action, in which he pits his clearer wits against those of Picklock, is Junior's device, and by setting up his own little scene and calling to witness an auditor who saw nothing but heard everything, he strips the mask from Picklock, restores order to a corrupted community, and both serves and rejoins his family. Peni-boy Senior will do so too, but not before he has taught a lesson to Block and Lollard, his rebellious dogs, for jumping up to, gnawing, and befouling his servants, instead of staying in their holes. The dogs' names pair Wycliffe's 'idle babblers' with an image of execution. Even their roles are taken over when like a latter-day Morose Peni-boy Senior suffers further vexatious baiting from the jeerers who burst in upon the trial scene.

Nevertheless, Jonson's play only contains all this; it is far from being one with it. In a sentence which he plants with a self-reflecting irony, he 'neuer did wrong, but with iust cause.' Even the prodigal theme is Canter's and the Gossips'. Jonson may seem to have altered the story, since it is the father who is thought to be dead, but of course that is not so: it is the son who was dead and by the end of the play is alive again. He may have seemed to depart from traditional forms ('That was the old way,' says Mirth), but the conventional wisdom of the parables is not outdated. Canter's stale sentences are news. Dramatically speaking, Jonson is not drawing farts out of dead bodies. Mirth may think that he has omitted beggarly heirs, poets, scholars, doctors, and sea captains, but Junior is a 'Begger in veluet' and Madrigal, Piedmantle, Almanack, and Shunfield fit the others to perfection. For Jonson is a creator of a feigned commonwealth and its beggars are all there. When he says that the Staple of News is a place 'wherin the age may see her owne folly' he means the news office, his own play, and the succession of plays made within it where spectators take the stage and in affirming their independence are made to display the ignorance of their judgment and their betrayal of true theatre. His dramatic structure creates its own proof. If we see it at all, we may think that Act IV is a masque, but of course it is a fully-developed antimasque which must come to an end before the family reunion can take place in Act V. As Mr Orgel says, 'for Jonson it was the antimasque that served to give meaning to the masque, to explain it, to make the audience understand.'[4] The play ends only as Peni-boy Senior gives away the bride to his nephew and joins their hands. It is a cue for Canter to say:

If the Spectators will joyne theirs, wee thanke 'hem.

and Junior to add:

And wish they may, as I, enioy Pecunia.

Paired with Junior and flanked by the brothers, Pecunia completes the tableau and both embodies and delivers its meaning.

The several levels of the action, like the receding planes of a toy theatre, also express with sharpening irony a hierarchy of values according to which the theatrical forms become more sophisticated and their substance more degenerate as we move in towards the masque. The apparent disparity between realistic and allegorical elements, like the varying density of the verse, is not a weakness but reflects with deliberate skill the several levels of apprehension appropriate to the forms. The true language of the play is in its powerfully co-ordinated structural statement, not in the odd speech. In this way too Jonson unites past and present theatre, and once we have seen that his ironic masque is a tissue of lies and his crude morality an instrument of truth, we then have to discount our conclusion, for Jonson's public play is larger than either the masque or the morality, and transcends both in the truth of its comment on the times.

These remarks about Jonson's organisation of the play in terms of dramatic depth and time should not obscure the more obvious surface unity, again consciously de-vised, of the Peni-boys, Pecunia, the Staplers, Jeerers, and nominees for the College of Canters. The links between the institutions have a basis in fact, but this is reinforced by ties of family and service, by the overlapping roles, especially those of Picklock, Cymbal, and Lickfinger, and by the actively integrative function of the news office in Act III. This jigsaw coherence is also expressed in the familiar Jonsonian construction of a representative world. The Staple itself is a comprehensive symbol for society, and, like the Stapler Cymbal, Jonson allots roles to his characters which, when related, account for most of its functions. Of course this reduction to type diminishes their humanity and credibility although this has been trebly justified. First, within the play their roles are self-created, even Canter's; second, they show the conse-quences of men abusing their own humanity (so Pick-lock, with forehead of steel and mouth of brass, is what he would be); third, where the characters constantly confuse art and reality and thereby lose the perspective necessary to knowledge, their very theatricality should prevent us from doing the same and ensure that we concentrate on the larger argument. The position is of course a Brechtian one, but the danger does not lie only in the audience's readiness to be distracted, for any actor would rather have the audience believe his character than view him as a mere contributor to an abstract design. Hence it is not surprising that several of Jonson's prefatory notes, especially that to *The New Inn*, suggest that he could do without actors.

Jonson's provision of a whole gallery of role-players is extended with perfect stylistic consistency to the staging itself. For *The Staple of News* is a play of shows. It works through costume, music, dance, display, and violent action, all of which call for brilliant visual staging. Its structure is ostensibly open and obvious and offers superb chances for ingenious use of stage space and lighting to express perspectives on the action and even audience-assault; it is an open invitation to a stage designer to display the symbolic characters literally larger than life, to show Pecunia as indeed a Venus of the time, with her banner-bearing prophets in their own poster-theatre act: *Pecunia omnia potest* and *Pecunia obediunt omnia*. Anyone who has been to recent Aldwych Theatre productions and experienced the auditorium lights going up during the act to force us on stage, or has seen the production by the same company of Genet's *The Balcony* with its outsize puppets, or had his hand shaken at the end of *A Midsummer Night's Dream*, can hardly doubt that *The Staple of News* is ripe for revival or that it would be brilliantly served by the Royal Shakespeare Company. Of course it would all be ironic, and Jonson would not thank one for defending his under-written characters by some formula which multiplied costume colour by length of stage exposure, but the irony would have a fine edge and one might be forgiven for suspecting that it was offered with both a genuine pride in the achievement of mounting such a show and disgust for the audience that enjoyed it.

I have scarcely touched on the thematic unity of the play, but in no other does Jonson offer to relate in such a penetrating and cohesive way economics and language as forces for binding or disrupting community. He had explored the relation of language to poetry in *The Poetaster* and that of language to government in *Cynthia's Revels*. In *Volpone* and *The Alchemist* he had exposed rhetoric as an index of diseased imagination and as a disguise for avarice, itself destructive of the true commonwealth. Only in *The Staple of News*, however, are the social uses of language fully explored. The consequences of man's readiness to pervert and exploit for gain his distinctive excellence are projected here in an impressively universal way in the Staple of News and the College of Canters as symbols of institutionalized corruption, and in the subversion of theatre as their victim in all its forms. The play itself, by contrast, sets out to show what drama can still do and how superior it is to the press as an instrument of political understanding.

In his epilogue Jonson expressed his hope that if the play should fail to please,

> *It will not be imputed to his wit.*
> *A* Tree *so tri'd, and bent, as 'twill not start.*
> *Nor doth he often cracke a string of Art ...*

Recognition of the play's artifice and therefore of his artistry is essential to Jonson's self-esteem, and for us to see the pattern is at once a compliment to him and a recognition of our own responsibility to act on the knowledge conveyed. Jonson's subtlety is such that it is virtually impossible to fault him. There is no lack of skill in *The Staple of News* and he has effectively undercut any criteria we might use to say so.

How to say then that both *The Staple of News* and any critique of it were alike bound to fail? Perhaps it is simply that the ingenuity is after all just too self-satisfying, that the social problem of news, like the critical comments we offer, is too much of Jonson's own making. Perhaps the simplifications, however well-informed by respectably acceptable values, never wholly escape nor truly place the denser life they seek to contain and define. A theory of humours requires a matching concession of diminished responsibility. Reformation, we recognise, is not meant to be enacted in fully human terms on stage, for the characters have no life but what we give them, and the demonstration suffices if it speaks to our minds and changes us. But Jonson's conservatism runs deep and the way it pervades his dramatic form suggests that he has little faith in man's capacity even to see the light, let alone follow it. The anger which he shows for the Staple may seem to spring from a concern for the people, but its effect is to abuse them for visiting this 'house of fame'

> *Where both the curious, and the negligent;*
> *The scrupulous, and careless; wilde, and stay'd;*
> *The idle, and laborious; all doe meet,*
> *To tast the* Cornu copiae *of her rumors,*
> *Which she, the mother of sport, pleaseth to scatter*
> *Among the vulgar: Baites, Sir, for the people!*
> *And they will bite like fishes.*
> [*The Staple of News*, iii.ii.115–22]

The moral earnestness comes close to the puritan intolerance he so berated in others. More seriously perhaps – and this gets close to the worrying problem of his artistic excellence – concern for his audience leads him into the devious ingenuity of the schizophrenic who plays off the real world with ironies, double-entendres, and situational games that permit him to keep his inner world intact while abusing his fellows with their forms. The late plays in particular become elaborate devices for proving the folly, irrelevant expectations, ignorant judgment, and false gratifications of his audiences. The final irony is that Peni-boy Canter *was* dead, and for all the brilliance of Jonson's redeeming arts, the theatre died with him. We return, past the irony of Expectation's words, to the simple truth that worried Jonson himself:

Absurdity on him, for a huge ouergrowne Play-maker! *why should he make him liue againe, when they, and we all thought him dead? If he had left him to his ragges, there had been an end of him.*
[*The Staple of News*, Fourth Intermean, 8–11]

The Staple of News is at once a supremely perceptive, intelligently argued, ingeniously structured comment on his times. In marking Jonson's return to the public stage it is also a courageous reaffirmation, deeply conservative but powerfully sanctioned, of the dramatic poet's public role as spokesman for his age, a role which the development of the press, with its unsifted reports and vulgarity of language, threatened to usurp. But for all its virtue, Jonson's response failed in one vital point: it shows no understanding at all of what a painful struggle it is for the ill-educated to learn a new language of conscience and independent political judgment. In deriding their attempts and shutting up his circle against them, Jonson sealed himself off from a world that was becoming uncomfortably intrusive, and in doing so he ceased to be a public poet.

It is only to be expected that the lover of true art and the enemies of all art, poet and puritan, will sometimes seem to speak with the same voice. Jonson's *Poetaster* and *Cynthia's Revels* make much of the paradox, and the false wit, empty rhetoric, parasitic acting, and visionary materialism of the middle plays are subtle variations on the same theme. But as a problem with both aesthetic and political implications it is most prominent in the period of Jonson's late plays.

The really trenchant expression of the puritan voice is Prynne's *Histrio-Mastix* of 1633, which had grown in bulk and vehemence in the three years it took to print. If Jonson was by then disenchanted with the court masque, his criticism was oblique and milky-hearted compared with that of Prynne, who took good example 'for all Pagan, all Christian Princes and Magistrates, to beware of being besotted with Plays, or Actors, as [one] prodigious Pagan Emperour & others were to their eternal infamy.' Nor did Prynne shrink from defining 'Women-Actors' as 'notorious whores' and from asking: 'dare then any Christian woman be so more than whorishly impudent, as to act, or speake publikely on a Stage ... ?'[5]

The day after the queen had acted in a pastoral, Laud, soon to be archbishop, showed the book to the king and queen, who were duly enraged; but more seriously Prynne was charged not only with railing upon Stageplays but with writing 'diverse incitements, to stir up the People to discontent, as if there were just cause to lay violent hands upon their Prince.'

At the same time the king let it be known that he wanted the Inns of Court to supply, in Bulstrode Whitelock's words, 'the outward and splendid visible testimony of a Royal Masque in evidence of his subjects' love,' for 'it was hinted at in the Court that this action would manifest the difference of their opinion from Mr. Prynne's new learning, and serve to confute his *Histrio Mastix* against enterludes.'

Shirley's *The Triumph of Peace* began as a procession headed by twenty footmen, followed by marshalls and officers and one hundred gentlemen of the Inns of Court mounted on the best horses and making 'the most glorious and splendid shew that ever was beheld in *England*.' Then came the antimasquers, the first being cripples and beggars on horseback, 'the poorest and leanest Jades that could be gotten out of the Dirt-carts.' More horsemen and an antimasque of projectors followed, among them a 'Fellow with a bunch of Carrots upon his Head, and a Capon upon his Fist, describing a *Projector* who begg'd a Patent of *Monopoly*, as the first Inventor of the Art to feed Capons fat with Carrots ...' And 'it pleased the Spectators the more, because by it an Information was covertly given to the King of the unfitness and ridiculousness of these Projects.' In the banqueting hall the masque was danced, played, sung, and spoken to perfection, and the queen and 'great Ladies were very free and civil in dancing with all the masquers.' They continued in their sports until it was almost morning, when there was a stately banquet; and thus, writes Whitelock, 'was this earthly Pomp and Glory, if not Vanity, soon past over and gone, as if it had never been.' The bill – over £21,000 – was real enough, but the queen's preferred consolation was 'that she never saw any Masque more noble.'[6]

My point here is that an attack on the theatre had been construed as a political attack on the king. The king's answer was to command a theatrical parade of remarkably self-betraying inanity and extravagance to establish the political fact, as he saw it, of his subjects' love. Instead of answering Prynne it ironically proved him right; and since it could hardly have been better calculated as a final rebuff to Jonson, it thrust puritan and poet into a paradoxical alliance.

In their view of the relationship of stage and state, William Prynne and Ben Jonson are in this sense two faces of the same coin. The court was not to be improved by plays and Jonson, like Prynne, knew too well now how it could be corrupted by them.

> *Playes in themselues have neither hopes, nor feares;*
> *Their fate is only in their hearers eares:*
>   [*The New Inn*, Epilogue]

Charles in any case had his own way of making men wise
by their ears. While Prynne was pilloried, his ears sliced
off, and his book burned – marking with a fine theatrical
flare the innovation of a custom hitherto unknown in
England – Jonson fiddled with *A Tale of a Tub*

> *to shew what different things*
> *The* Cotes *of* Clownes, *are from the* Courts *of* Kings.
>   [*A Tale of a Tub*, Prologue]

The radical judgment on a corrupt state as imaged in
its theatre is not Jonson's but Prynne's, as Laud and the
king recognised. Jonson holds to his vision of an ordered
society purged of folly and greed, and however bitter
his resentment of failure or of 'Spectacles of State' sup-
planting his 'more remou'd *mysteries*,' he is inescapably
committed to the court and is one with it in accepting its
position of privileged exclusiveness and its policy of suppression in defiance of new voices. The imagery of his
attack on Alexander Gill, who had dared to criticise *The
Magnetic Lady* –

> *A Rogue by Statute, censur'd to be whipt,*
> *Cropt, branded, slit, neck-stockt; go, you are stript.*

– is less revealing for the indignation it expresses than
for its endorsement of institutionalised barbarities. If
Charles could fire the devil from Prynne's pages, Jonson
was not above calling in Vulcan to second his execration
of Jones:

> *Lyue long the Feasting Roome. And ere thou burne*
> *Againe, thy Architect to ashes turne!*
> *Whom not ten fyres, nor a Parlyament can*
> *With all Remonstrance make an honest man.*
>   ['*An Expostulacion with Inigo Jones*,' 101–4]

Even conceding the impossibility of reforming this sur-
veyor of the king's works and architect of the Banqueting
Hall, there is little faith there in the efficacy of parlia-
ments. Charles had ensured in March 1629 that his went
into a long recess; in October 1632 'Stationers, Printers
and Booke Sellers' were prohibited by a Star Chamber
decree from printing and publishing 'the ordinary Gazetts
and Pamphletts of newes';[7] and in 1633 the Master of
the Revels even required that old plays be recensored,
'since they may be full of offensive things against church
and state, ye rather that in former time the poetts tooke
greater liberty than is allowed them by mee.'[8]

Neither puritans, painters, parliamentarians, nor printers would have had much sympathy from Jonson, but
neither was the court any longer one to shelter or respect
him. It was futile to hope for reform from a mediocre
monarch and since Jonson had no audience that he could
respect it was equally futile to satirise the travesty of
courtliness and good government that he observed. Like
Ginsberg in his poem 'America' Jonson, when he would
talk to his country, found that he was talking to himself.

The Staple of News is the hardening point of Jonson's
isolation, and the wholly derisive view he presents of a
stupid audience, gullible populace, and false educators,
fed by a staple diet of Bourne and Butter, is logically cli-
maxed by a symbolic act of suppression – which is only
the mirror image of wishful thinking – in the destruction
of the news office. His failure to see the potentialities for
good of an emergent medium, in reflecting more fully
than ever before the actual composition of the common-
wealth in the very diversity of its opinion and the pressure of its barely articulated strivings, is not so much a
failure of political awareness in itself as of artistic and
human sympathy, and *therefore* of political awareness.
Artistic because the society – the material, not the games
he played with it – is more complex than he represents it

to be, human because he cannot allow that a passionate sense of the self can be other than destructive. Humours are 'the root of all Schisme, and Faction, both in Church and Common-wealth,' says Probee in *The Magnetic Lady*.[9] Like an informant reporting in 1668, Jonson probably would have agreed that 'Conscience is made a cloak for ignorance, wilfulness and treachery. These people are children in understanding, but men in malice.'[10] By contrast, someone like William Prynne, despite the burning of his book about the theatre and the loss of his ears, knows of and speaks to a large class within a new and politically influential order, albeit, as his prosecutor affirmed, in 'all the vile Terms ... of the Oyster women at Billingsgate, or at the Common Conduit.'[11]

I have said enough to show that Jonson did not let the sword sleep in his hand. His efforts to write a drama for his own times are clearly seen in his formal innovations and are explicit in the way he supersedes older theatrical forms in the very act of using them anew. But his movement is ineluctably elitist and escapist. The jeerers are expelled and the world of every day is left to Fly and his crew. As he moves towards pastoral he romanticises his lower characters and their rural settings, employs dialect and folk motifs, preluding his retreat in space and time to Sherwood Forest and a distant 'Landt-shape of Forrest, Hils, Vallies, Cottages, A Castle, A River, Pastures, Heards, Flocks, all full of Countrey simplicity': in the words of a great teacher of our own day, 'an organic community with the living culture it embodied' where one might find 'an art of life, a way of living, ordered and patterned, involving social arts, codes of intercourse and a responsive adjustment, growing out of immemorial experience, to the natural environment and rhythm of the year';[12] where all evil is compressed at last, as at first in such a paradise, in a single figure outside the self, the witch Maudlin.

Failed by court or university, audience or students, Jonson evidences the same virtues and limitations of all whose passionate defence of minority culture is beyond criticism so long as it remains in a condition of high-minded self-abstraction from mass civilisation. However intemperate he might be, there is no questioning his integrity; as a teacher and dramatist he was courageous and ingenious in finding ways of mediating his values in forms all too capable of abuse by virtue of their public nature and in offering an imaginative reconstruction of British society which would make possible a life lived finely and responsibly. Neither the tone of the 'Ode to himself' and the 'Dedication, To the Reader' of *The New Inn*, nor his quarrel with Inigo Jones, should too easily divert us from the broader sympathy and generosity of spirit which the last plays show. They are not adequate to the problems he faces, his concern for people suffers from the artistic refinement which he so earnestly pursues, and his strategy of reformation is too cerebral to affect the court, too impersonal to strike the heart. But the concern goes deep and the skill to serve it is so seriously and dutifully offered that its rejection must have caused Jonson unimaginable pain.

> *But doe him right*
> *He meant to please you: for he sent things fit,*
> *In all the numbers, both of sense and wit.*
> [*The New Inn*, Epilogue]

And he never failed in intelligence:

> *All that this faint and faltring tongue doth crave*
> *Is, that you not impute it to his braine,*
> *That's yet unhurt, although set round with paine,*
> *It cannot long hold out.* [*Ibid.*]

We should do him wrong to buttress our own cynicism or sociological self-righteousness by wrenching out of shape a fine play like *The New Inn* and converting it into a bitter attack on the false court or a parody of the absurdities of romantic comedy. It has such things in it, but it moves seriously and with deliberation towards a transformation scene which, in a most sophisticated act of theatre, offers to create within us an apprehension of the virtues that should inform our conduct and of the beauty which illumines the sensuous world that we inhabit. In this play Jonson creates a mode of discourse close to pastoral, and because he allows the relation between art and life, between literary experience and social action, to be less direct, more mysterious, he evades the test of literal truth.

> LOV. *Is this a dreame now, after my first sleepe?*
> *Or are these phant'sies made i'the light Heart?*
> *And sold i'the new Inne?* HOST. *Best goe to bed,*
> *And dreame it ouer all.*
> [*The New Inn*, v.v.120–3]

The end of the play exists at the shadow-line of dream and waking, and when with the play behind them the characters '*goe out, with a* Song' they invest the articulated vision of poetry with the even more comprehensive harmonies of a music heard but not seen.

> *Where* should *this music be? i'the'air, or the'earth?*

asked Shakespeare's Ferdinand. But Jonson's Lovel finds beauty in the palpable world of

> *A skeine of silke, without a knot!*
> *A faire march made without a halt!*
> *A curious forme without a fault!*
> *A printed booke without a blot! ...*
> [*The New Inn*, iv.iv.9–12]

and his poem sanctifies the most intimate union of sense and spirit when he offers it

> to light us all to bed, 'twill be instead
> Of ayring of the sheets with a sweet odour.
>   [Ibid., v.v.151–2]

There is nothing escapist about pastoral as such. At its best it places the feverish world of politics and restores a sense of the deeper rhythms of life which politics should serve. And in any case there is a toughness of experience in and beyond *The New Inn* which gives Jonson every right to his romantic close:

> I am he
> Have measur'd all the Shires of England over,
> Wales, and her mountaines, seene those wilder nations,
> Of people in the Peake, and Lancashire;
> Their Pipers, Fidlers, Rushers, Puppet-masters,
> Iuglers and Gipseys, all the sorts of Canters,
> And Colonies of Beggars, Tumblers, Ape-carriers;
> For to these sauages I was addicted,
> To search their natures, and make odde discoveries!
>   [Ibid., v.v.93–100]

Of *The New Inn* Professor Bentley was probably right to say 'That the play deserved to fail in production can scarcely be doubted by any theatre-wise reader,'[13] for the art of theatre is rougher than sometimes, fondly, we imagine. Whatever the seriousness of Jonson's intention or the care he took to structure the event, it was no proof against drunken, tired, or disagreeable audiences, for which there is more evidence than for the intuition of solemn truths. And he felt himself triply betrayed this time for, if the king's subjects proved squeamish and censorious beholders, the King's Servants seemed also to have lost their integrity because *The New Inn* 'was neuer acted, but most negligently play'd,' and the court performance was cancelled.

The play is finer than much criticism or its all too brief theatrical history suggest, but the brute fact of its failure is proof of a kind that Jonson's dream of a degenerate monarchy transfigured, or of a factious and schismatic society reconciled, was incapable of realisation even as an image 'devis'd and play'd to take spectators.'

> *It was a beauty that I saw,*
> *So pure, so perfect, as the frame*
> *Of all the universe was lame,*
> *To that one figure, could I draw,*
> *Or give least line of it a law!*
> [*The New Inn*, iv.iv.4–8]

There's a touching note of incomprehension there which is part of the mystery itself, but it is not far either from political bewilderment. Cruelly deceived in his hopes of a judicious hearing, Jonson turned again to his readers.

> *How-so-ever, if thou canst but spell, and ioyne my sense, there is more hope of thee, than of a hundred fastidious* impertinents, *who were there present the first day* ...
> [*The New Inn*, Dedication, To the Reader]

Plagued by illness and a dilatory and careless printer, Jonson was again to be disappointed. *The New Inn* appeared but his projected second folio collection of 1631 proved abortive, and his hopes of those who could but spell cannot have been profound. For in *The Staple of News* he had already diagnosed the ills of this society in terms of a populace seduced by its own curiosity into a dizzy search for novelty, dazzled and mesmerised by surface display in dress and theatre, betrayed of its birthright by the economic exploitation of language in corrupting imitation of the public riot, and educated away from virtue and knowledge by an unholy alliance of business interests, professional ambitions, and colleges of higher learning. It sounds like a powerful and relevant indictment, and there is behind it a generalised concern for people that would save them from themselves.

For your owne sakes, not his, he bad me say,
Would you were come to heare, not see, a Play.
[*The Staple of News*, Prologue for the Stage]

Modern instances seem only to confirm its truth:

films, newspapers, publicity in all its forms, commerci-
ally-catered fiction – all offer satisfaction at the lowest
level, and inculcate the choosing of the most immediate
pleasures, got with the least effort.[14]

Like the theatre in Jonson's time, films

provide now the main form of recreation in the civilised
world; and they involve surrender under conditions of
hypnotic receptivity, to the cheapest emotional appeals,
appeals the more insidious because they are associated
with compellingly vivid illusions of actual life.

Such a culture is disseminated by economic and literal
mechanics and

it is vain to resist the triumph of the machine. It is equally
vain to console us with the promise of a 'mass culture'
that shall be utterly new. It would, no doubt, be possible
to agree that such a 'mass culture' might be better than
the culture we are losing, but it would be futile: the
'utterly new' surrenders everything that can interest us.[15]

Jonson may cry 'Come, leave the loathed Stage,' but he
finds no consolation outside in 'the more loathsome Age'
where

> *'Twere simple fury, still thy selfe to wast*
> *On such as have no taste!*
> ['*Ode to Himselfe*,' ll. 13–14]

Although he is aware from his own experience that no
man is so lowly that he may not grow in both virtue and
authority, Jonson adheres to court ideals and reverts to

ridicule and sarcastic summation of this other England. But political ideas in their popular form will rarely be expressed initially through rational debate and any expectation he had of the conscious restoration of an ordered, equitable, and single-minded society in an atomistic England was a pathetic illusion. He tried, with some success, to make his stage a speaking picture, but it went against the grain and he could never fully accept that demonstration was a dramatic language and therefore a political one too for those who had no other or for whom the existing one was obsolete. It is a truth that Shakespeare's Volumnia would have put to use:

> *Action is eloquence, and the eyes of the ignorant*
> *More learned than the ears.*
> *[Coriolanus, III.ii.76–7]*

But Jonson can ask nothing kindly of the crowd because he can only will its dissolution. It is no accident that in commenting on Shakespeare's mingled drama and saying that there is always an appeal open from criticism to nature, Jonson's namesake should observe that 'the high and the low co-operate in the general system by unavoidable concatenation.'

For if *The Staple of News* appears from one point of view to be an accurate forecast of a disastrous economic and cultural conspiracy, and singularly percipient in seeing an organised news network run for profit as the quite new phenomenon of a mass medium with comprehensive social and political consequences, from another point of view, like all the late plays, it too clearly shows the thoroughly reactionary nature of Jonson's political idealism. The voice that speaks truthfully both to its own times and to the embryonic future is that raised against the paternalistic spirit with its own limiting preconceptions:

Nor is it to the common people less than a reproach; for

if we be so jealous over them, as that we dare not trust
them with an English pamphlet, what doe we but censure
them for a giddy, vitious, and ungrounded people; in
such a sick and weak estate of faith and discretion as to
be able to take nothing down but through the pipe of a
licencer. That this is care or love of them, we cannot pre-
tend ...

[*Areopagitica* (1644), 23]

The pasteboard eloquence of the later masques was
more self-revealing than even Jonson dared to believe.
So too was the popular press. As an indicator of 'the body
of the time, his form and pressure,' it mirrored more faithfully and in a richer dialectic than could Jonson's attenu-
ated formalism and abstracted values the diversity of an
England stirring at last to protest more openly against
religious intolerance and political, social, and economic
privilege, and struggling to define in a quite new way the
nature of political responsibility. Jonson does not allow
himself this density of material, nor therefore a corresponding complexity of analysis. Paradoxically, the deli-
berative ingenuity of his dramatic structure, instead of
serving a deeper artistic compulsion, now inhibits it, as
though the frame were more important than the mirror
and order the one desperate necessity.

Truth's 'first appearance to our eyes bleared and dim-
med with prejudice and custom is more unsightly and
unplausible than many errors,' said Milton. The language
of Jonson's jeerers is a crude caricature of an emergent
dialogue by means of which the full range of the society,
and the nature of the necessary accommodation, were at
last *knowable*.[16]

In *News from the New World* Jonson had distinguished
printer from factor. It was the latter who hoped

to erect a Staple for newes ere long, whether all shall be
brought and thence againe vented under the name of

119

Staple-newes ... [for] it is the Printing I am offended at, I would have no newes printed; for when they are printed they leave to bee newes; while they are written, though they be false, they remaine newes still. [II.45–7, 57–60]

The point is a neat way of relating news to opinion and rumour; it has its own predictive relevance to the ephemerality of some visual and aural media-content of our own time; and it is taken over into the later play. But the more important perception is Jonson's awareness of a development within the book trade separating artisan printers from entrepreneurial booksellers and an equation of freedom of the Company with investment in its stock, made up largely of textbook copyrights. When shareholders in the Staple combine in turn with the jeerers to staff the College of Canters, he completes with perfect consistency the link between economic freedom, capital investment, and education.

Just as the popular press was a reflection of an egalitarian movement, and immensely educative in forming a new language for talking about politics, so too developments in education outside the two universities and the Inns of Court were the natural expression of an independence of mind in religion and science for the forms of which Jonson had little sympathy. Lectureships in particular flourished in the 1620s. And Jonson's professional jeerers in their university of the air of 1626 are not far removed in time or style from the lecturers whom Charles called 'furious promoters of the most dangerous innovations' or those who, for Laud in 1629, 'by reason of their pay are the people's creatures and blow the bellows of their sedition.'[17]

More striking however is the parallel between the College of Canters and Gresham College, founded by a merchant, administered jointly by the City and the Mercers' Company, not by the Church, with lectures in Eng-

lish delivered 'In the most perspicuous method,' not as
textual exegesis, and shaped with an absence of pedantry
'to the good liking and capacity of the hearers.'[18] There
were seven professorships which, in their traditional
number at least if not in all subjects, parallel those nomi-
nated for the College of Canters, as well as one moiety of
the Staple parts.[19] Jonson's attitude to Gresham College
must have been equivocal since many of his friends were
associated with it and he himself may have lectured there
on rhetoric in 1623. But it is hard to resist the conclusion
that its religious affiliations, openness to practical learning and scientific demonstration, its economic auspices
and popular pitch, were signs of a pragmatism too much
at odds with his own vision of society for Jonson to
tolerate.

These developments in news services and education
that Jonson had seen fit to link dignified their audiences.
By contrast, and fearful of popular influence on government, Jonson vilified them. But the culture needed to
yield men of good judgment is not easily acquired and is
scarcely available at all to most. To plead its necessity as
a form of exclusion is a common strategy of established
authority against aspirant power, perhaps simply of middle age against youth. The argument is sound in everything except a sympathetic sense of the pressures it ex-
cludes and can no longer quite control. Despite his formal
innovations, what Jonson and perhaps criticism of him
most lack here, in the moment of arguing for it, is a supple
political language adequate to the times, and his conservative sympathies lead him away from its possibilities
rather than towards them. Such a language was shaped
in the years that followed, but it would be naive to think
that its fine flowering in the writings of a Clarendon,
Hobbes, Harrington, or Winstanley owed nothing to the
developments in publishing and teaching which Jonson
derides, for these were its undergrowth where the expres-

sion of particular conflicting needs, political, economic, and spiritual, sharpened moral awareness and created tensions which gave a fine edge to judgment.

Since Jonson insists on his function as teacher and on the relation between his feigned society and the real one, and since he exposes Nathaniel Butter to such heatedly withering ridicule that he ought simply to have melted away, it may not be such a naive question to ask whether that sounding brass, the press, symbol of mass ignorance, did anything but

deride
The wretched; or with buffon *licence ieast*
At whatsoe'r is serious, if not sacred.
[*The Staple of News*, v.vi.9–11]

Leafing quickly through some news-sheets of early 1622, I came upon the following passage. It is not great and it has its point of view, but like that of many fine sermons in the period its focus is community, not conquest, and it would not disgrace the pages of our liberal press today in its concern to drive beyond partisan views to describe the ravages of war and the plight of those caught in it. The Dutch imprint on this news pamphlet is almost certainly spurious and it was probably printed by Edward Allde, one of several printers used by Bourne, Butter, and Archer to transmit such trifles through the barriers of censorship in order to satisfy the curiosity of their customers in 'a weekly cheat to draw mony.'

By the occasion of these warres, and dilacerating the peace and plenty of Countries, this goodly Prouince of the Palatinate had come into the hands of cruell vsurpers, and vnnatural strangers, who haue respected nothing, but the present time, and supplying of wants, not caring what became of her hereafter, nor how deformed they made her for to welcome her owne parents: For they cut downe

122

her Woods, even before Franckendale, and other places, to preuent annoyance from the Enemy, who kept in the same as vnder shelter, and from thence made many sallyes vpon the people, and lay as it were in Ambuscado to surprise the Souldiers: they ouertrampled her Vines, and made the hoofes of their Horses speake cruelly to the rootes: they digged vp her fields for Trenches and Bulwarks: they pulled downe their houses round about their Townes to raise rauelings and counterscarps, they oppressed the people, suffering no man to enioy his owne, nor to giue it away to whom they pleased: so that they which before in a manner liued securely without walls, and fortifications, are not now safe within walls, trenches, and the mounting of Cannons: and this is the misery of discention, and the rage of Princes, who will not be pacified without mischiefe and reuenge, as is apparant all ouer Bohemia and those Countries, where the Enemies haue come in with the sound of hostility.[20]

Again we might do worse than seek honest comment from Dr Johnson, who said that 'wit can stand its ground against truth only a little while,' and compound that remark with another in his *Essay on the Origin and Importance of Small Tracts and Fugitive Pieces* which recognised that 'In such writings may be seen how the mind has been opened by degrees ...'[21]

Jonson is agile in self-defence and although he had to append a note to the readers of *The Staple of News* to insist on his allegory, he had already built in a defensive device in Canter's words:

> *If thou had'st sought out good and vertuous persons*
> *Of these professions: I'had lou'd thee and them:*
> *For these shall neuer have that plea 'gainst me,*
> *Or colour of aduantage, that I hate*
> *Their callings, but their manners, and their vices.*
> [*The Staple of News,* IV.iv.135–9]

Canter's catalogue of professions makes no provision, however, for the role of the press as a public teacher, and in the note to the readers to which I have just referred Jonson makes clear his complete rejection of its right to any such function. The contrast he draws is not between a responsible and an irresponsible press, but between poets and news-vendors, ideal truth and that literal falsehood or competing fantasy of news made like

the times Newes, (*a weekly cheat to draw mony*) *and* [it] *could not be fitter reprehended, then in raising this ridiculous* Office *of the* Staple, *wherein the age may see her owne folly, or hunger and thirst after* [not righteousness, but] *publish'd pamphlets of* Newes, *set out euery Saturday, but made all at home, & no syllable of truth in them: then which there cannot be a greater disease in nature, or a fouler scorne put vpon the times. And so apprehending it, you shall doe the* Author, *and your owne iudgement a courtesie, and perceiue the tricke of alluring money to the* Office, *and there cooz'ning the people. If you haue the truth, rest quiet, and consider that*
　　　Ficta, voluptatis causa, sint proxima veris.

The sinister interpretation which Jonson was at pains to discount must have found parallels not only between 'Aurelia Clara Pecunia, the Infanta' and the Infanta of Spain, but between the prodigal Pennyboy Junior and Charles I, who assumed his full patrimony with his coronation robes on 2 February 1626, only a week or two before the play was performed. Given that, it is not at all difficult to spin a fanciful web in which the abortive Spanish match casts the glittering Buckingham as Cymbal in a group of Charles's false friends, the discord between Pennyboy Canter and Pennyboy Junior mirrors that between the late king and the prince, the abuse of Pecunia directly symbolises prostitution of the court masque (itself a measure of economic profligacy), Pennyboy Canter images the death and hopeful resurrection of James I in posthumous admonishment of his errant son, and even the dead Prince Henry, the elder brother of the parable, is present – by being absent.

> ... *though they are not truths, th'innocent* Muse
> *Hath made so like, as Phant'sie could them state,*
> *Or* Poetry, *without scandall, imitate.*
> [*The Staple of News*, Prologue for the Court]

Happily we have to reject these speculations: quite apart from Jonson's admonition and Mirth's salutary example, there is too little scholarly evidence and there are too many inconsistencies. Nevertheless they sharpen the platitude that Jonson saw his role as that of a serious public commentator observing quite concrete events whose underlying pattern it was his duty to discern, restructure, criticise, and realise in a public form.

> *All that dable in the inke,*
> *And defile quills, are not those few, can thinke,*
> *Conceiue, expresse, and steere the soules of men,*
> *As with a rudder, round thus, with their pen.*
> [*The Staple of News*, Prologue for the Stage]

But those who dabbled in the ink were no longer simply poetasters like Madrigal, seeking a false reputation as artists by turning a vacuous lyric with merely technical skill. They were reporters of public events, and the conflicting information they offered, the variety of motive and opinion, shifted the burden of interpretation to the individual himself. Without the dramatist's powers of analysis and recreation he may have been most faint, but what strength he had *was* his own. The development of political responsibility in the seventeenth century, of which Jonson's audience games are a negative image, is inseparable from the growth of a new public function for the press and its writers. This is why the animus against mere news is central to Jonson's conception of the play and why it is not to be subordinated to some more abstracted, if formally unifying, theme. In a sense true of none of the other late plays, although they show its consequences, *The Staple of News* marks the end of theatre as the only secular mass medium, the end of the playhouse as the principal forum of public debate, the end of the actors' popular function as the abstracts and brief chronicles of the time. The dramatic poet, as rhetor in the truest sense, had lost his vocation to a journalist.

NOTES

1 L.C. Knights, *Drama and Society in the Age of Jonson* (London 1937), 220
2 *Ben Jonson*, ed. C.H. Herford and P.E. Simpson, 11 vols (Oxford 1925–52), IV, 178
3 L.C. Knights, 222
4 S. Orgel, *The Jonsonian Masque* (Cambridge, Mass. 1967), 93
5 *Histrio-Mastix* (1633), 709 and index, art. 'Women-Actors'
6 Bulstrode Whitelock, *Memorials of the English Affairs* (1682), 18–21
7 Folke Dahl, *A Bibliography of English Corantos and Periodical Newsbooks 1620–1642* (London 1952), 19
8 *The Dramatic Records of Sir Henry Herbert*, ed. J.Q. Adams (New Haven 1917), 21
9 Samuel Johnson: 'It is to be observed, that, among the Natives of *England*, is to be found a greater Variety of Humour, than in any other Country; and, doubtless, where every Man has a full Liberty to propagate his Conceptions, Variety of Humour must produce Variety of Writers; and, where the Number of Authors is so great, there cannot but be some worthy of Distinction.' *An Essay on the Origin and Importance of Small Tracts and Fugitive Pieces*, reprinted in *A Miscellany of Tracts and Pamphlets*, ed. A.C. Ward (Oxford 1927), 387

10 Public Record Office, London, *State Papers* (Domestic Series), 8 January 1668

11 J. Rushworth, *Historical Collections*, 7 vols (1650–1701), II, 220ff

12 F.R. Leavis and Denys Thompson, *Culture and Environment* (London 1933), 150

13 G.E. Bentley, *The Jacobean and Caroline Stage*, 7 vols (London 1941–6), IV, 623

14 Leavis and Thompson, 3

15 F.R. Leavis, *Mass Civilisation and Minority Culture* (London 1930), 9–10, 30. The last sentiment is close to that of Henry James in a letter to William, who had recommended a 'Newspaporial' bearing: 'The multitude, I am more and more convinced, has absolutely no taste – none at least that a thinking man is bound to defer to.' See Leon Edel, *Henry James: The Conquest of London 1870–1883* (London 1962), 71.

16 Jonson and Milton both pay their tributes to Selden, but for Milton he is 'the chief of learned men reputed in this Land ... whose volume of naturall & national laws proves, not only by great authorities brought together, but by exquisite reasons and theorems almost mathematically demonstrative, that all opinions, yea, errors, known, read, and collated, are of main service & assistance toward the speedy attainment of what is truest.' (*Areopagitica*, 11)

17 Christopher Hill, *The Century of Revolution 1603–1714* (London 1972), 83–5, 145

18 *An Account of the Rise, Foundation, Progress and Present State of Gresham College in London* (1707), passim. A convenient and informative discussion is that by Christopher Hill in *The Intellectual Origins of the English Revolution* (London 1972), 34–61. For Jonson's association with Gresham College see Herford and Simpson XI, 582–5, and C. J. Sisson, *Times Literary Supplement*, 21 September 1951. I am grateful to Professor L.A. Beaurline for suggesting the connection with *The Staple of News*.

19 At I.v.106–8 Cymbal says that he has 'the iust *moyetie*' for his part in the news office and that the other moiety is

divided into seven parts. If, as Herford and Simpson suggest (II,173–5), Cymbal is modelled on Captain Thomas
Gainsford, this would leave the other moiety in the hands
of the booksellers. Of the seven parts, six were full shares
and one was divided into two half-shares. In the extant
news pamphlets for the period 1622–6 six names, and only
six names, frequently recur: those of Nathaniel Butter,
Thomas Archer, Nicholas Bourne, William Sheffard, Bartholomew Downes, and Nathaniel Newbury. This actual
syndicate corresponds very closely to the structure of
Jonson's Staple. There could well have been a seventh part
too, but its subdivision would have given the two shareholders only a small part in the venture and their names
would be unlikely to appear in the imprints.

20 *Newes from the Palatinate,* 'Printed at the Hage. 1622,'
   10–11. There can be no doubt of course that the object of
   the news report was to inform and strengthen protestant
   opinion in England and to secure James's intervention in
   the Palatinate.

21 Loc. cit., 388–9

'A MORE SECRET *CAUSE*': THE WIT OF JONSON'S POETRY

HUGH MACLEAN

The standing of Jonson's poetry on the critical baro-
meter, over the last century or so, may be said to have
come right about from 'Storm' to 'Set Fair.' Macaulay,
gloomily contemplating what he called 'the jagged mis-
shapen distichs' of Jonson's couplets, thought that they
resembled 'blocks rudely hewn out by an unpractised
hand, with a blunt hatchet';[1] Sir Walter Scott recoiled
from Jonson's 'coarseness of taste,' noting his unhappy
predilection for 'filthy and gross ... pleasantry' as a 'sin
against decorum.'[2] Swinburne, lamenting that 'so great
an English writer as Ben Jonson should ever have taken
the plunge of a Parisian diver into the cesspool,' maintained the inalienable right of English readers to 'agree ...
that coprology should be left to Frenchmen.'[3] But the
critics of our own time, not much moved by such *jeux
d'esprit* as 'The Famous Voyage,' have brought Jonson's
poetry back into the light. It was Professor Knights who
observed, in 1937, that 'the appreciation of Ben Jonson
starts from the appreciation of his verse'; F.R. Leavis

subsequently placed Jonson at the spring-head of that
'line of wit' which led on to Pope; while the work of
Trimpi, Walton, and Spanos (with others) has significantly helped in the developing recognition that Jonson
is 'an important poet' by virtue of 'his integrity to the
experience he is trying to communicate, the honesty of
the matter-and-manner relationship in his verse, and his
notable sense of linguistic appropriateness.'[4] The purpose
of this paper is to make some suggestions bearing on the
wit of Jonson's poetry, noticing particularly its intriguing
combination of freedom and control, in terms of Jonson's
critical stance and of his attention to that decorum which
implies, as Joseph Summers has observed in another connection, 'that harmony is natural to man and that man is
more than the sum of his activities.'[5]

For Jonson, of course, to be truly a poet is also to be
(with much else besides) a critic, of society as well as
poetry. Some men, he observes,

thinke no Learning good, but what brings in gaine. ...
But, if an other Learning, well used, can instruct to good
life, informe manners; no lesse perswade, and leade men,
then they threaten, and compell; and have no reward:
is it therefore the worse study? ... that he which can faine
a Common-wealth *(which is the* Poet) *can governe it with*
Counsels, *strengthen it with* Lawes, *correct it with*
Judgements, *informe it with* Religion, *and* Morals; *is all*
these. Wee do not require in him meere Elocution; *or an*
excellent faculty in verse; but the exact knowledge of all
vertues, and their Contraries; with ability to render the
one lov'd, the other hated, by his proper embattaling
them.[6]

To take under consideration the range of Jonson's critical
pronouncements is forcibly to be reminded of a number
of celebrated passages in the prose of John Milton. To

begin with, we are confronted with the figure who, impatient of fugitive and cloistered virtues, prefers (and delights in) the dust and heat of the arena, where he may limn 'the times deformitie ... With constant courage, and contempt of feare.'[7] The character of Asper is 'eager and constant in reproofe'; while Mercury, the 'sacred god of wit,' approves that 'exempt, and only man-like course' adopted by Crites, whose satiric art at length enforces the wayward courtiers to acknowledge that they 'merit sharpe correction.'[8] Making every allowance for Jonson's recognition that, properly speaking, 'men judge only out of knowledge. That is the trying faculty,' that the true critic has nothing to do with 'particular, and private spleene,' and that, in 'quick *comoedie*, refined,' the critic of poetry and society will be effective in proportion as he employs sportive indirection, one is regularly impressed by the forthright vigour and primitive energy of Jonson's critical pronouncements.[9] It is chiefly in *Every Man Out of His Humour*, *Cynthia's Revels*, and *The Poetaster*, perhaps, that one is made aware of the combative aspect of the critic's function. Over the whole range of Jonson's comic drama, however, 'the modest anger of a *satyricke* spirit'[10] is regularly brought to bear on fops, rhymesters, fools, and knaves.

All that fierceness is expended in the cause of 'making the citizens better' (as Aristophanes had put it); in *The Devil is an Ass*, Manly observes that those few at least who 'have the seeds / Of goodnesse left,' induced by the satirist's art to feel shame, may consequently 'make their way / To a true life.'[11] A passage more directly relevant here, however, is the account of the satirist's aim given by Crites. Noting that men possess 'Such powers of wit, and soule, as are of force / To raise their beings to aeternitie,' he undertakes to render these powers more than merely potential; to develop, in fact,

An inward comelinesse of bountie, knowledge,
And spirit, that may conforme them, actually,
To Gods high figures, which they have in power ...[12]

That is to say, he enables men to realize full 'inward ripeness.' But this high task is effectively reserved for the true poet and critic, who exemplifies the virtues he would evoke from others. As Milton would observe, in *Smectymnuus*, that the poet 'ought himself to be a true poem; that is, a composition and pattern of the best and honourablest things,' so Jonson insists that 'if men will impartially, and not a-squint, looke toward the offices, and function of a Poet, they will easily conclude to themselves, the impossibility of any mans being the good Poet, without first being a good man.'[13] Crites is described as

A creature of a most perfect and divine temper. ... Hee strives rather to bee that which men call judicious, then to bee thought so: and is so truly learned, that he affects not to show it. Hee will thinke, and speake his thought, both freely: but as distant from depraving another mans merit, as proclaiming his owne. ... In summe, he hath a most ingenuous and sweet spirit, a sharp and season'd wit, a straight judgment, and a strong mind. Fortune could never breake him, nor make him lesse.[14]

Such a paragon will, no doubt, regularly exercise his wit and judgment in the lists of critical and literary combat; but he will also, perhaps even chiefly, fulfill his role as poet and critic by being what he is: by demonstrating, *in esse*, that range and totality of virtue which may be attained by other men, aroused and given purpose by his example. Clearly, to apply the term 'dynamic' exclusively to the poet and critic in his overtly combative role is inappropriate, since the natural energies that inform his character enable this 'master in manners' to teach 'things divine, no lesse then humane,' and to 'effect the businesse of man-kind.'[15] Perhaps it is not altogether fanciful to recall, by way of analogy, Henry Adams' account of those two kinds of energy, the humming forty-foot dynamos (which Adams certainly felt to be 'a moral force'), and the still Virgin, whose power encompassed 'emotion, human expression, beauty, purity.'[16]

It seems to be true that the plays show forth Jonson primarily in his actively combative role, concerned with 'the satiric recognition and description of those factors that contribute to social disorder,'[17] and eager in the cause of persuading an audience to recognize and condemn the various shortcomings of those who are taxed by the author's 'sports.' It is chiefly in the non-dramatic verse, by contrast, that Jonson comes before his readers in that other aspect of the poet's role. I am not suggesting that Jonson everywhere and exclusively adopts one stance in the plays and another in the non-dramatic pieces; a good many of the *Epigrammes* are obviously combative *in excelsis*, to say nothing of such poems as 'A Little Shrub Growing By.' Again, certain of the verse-epistles are effective largely by virtue of the ferocious relish informing Jonson's account of the giddy society that presses in upon such images of heroic virtue as Lady Aubigny or the Countess of Rutland. But I think it may generally be granted that if, in the plays, the poet and critic is identified with that man whose 'strict hand / Was made to ceaze on vice,' in the non-dramatic verse one more often observes a figure 'Who (like a circle bounded in it selfe) / Contaynes as much, as man in fulnesse may.'[18]

To acknowledge so much is certainly not to conclude that Jonson's purposes as poet and critic are, in the plays, cramped and negative, in the non-dramatic poetry positive and full. It seems to be arguable, however, that the index of his stature in this double role, namely that elusive quality we call Jonson's wit, is displayed in the verse with at least as intriguing a variety and amplitude as is the case in the plays, and that this has something to do with the shape of decorum that obtains in much of the non-dramatic verse. By way of paradox, although when Jonson's capacity to enchant or excite is in question one is apt to think first of those delightful or savage dramatic compositions, it is particularly the non-dramatic verse in which the poet-critic may be observed 'at play' in the fullest sense. 'Man is made God's plaything,' Plato observes in the *Laws*,

> *and that is the best part of him. Therefore every man and woman should live life accordingly, and play the noblest games and be of another mind from what they are at present. ... What, then, is the right way of living? Life must be lived as play, playing certain games, making sacrifices, singing and dancing, and then a man will be able to propitiate the gods, and defend himself against his enemies, and win in the contest.*[19]

As Huizinga remarks, 'In play we may move below the level of the serious, as the child does; but we can also move above it – in the realm of the beautiful and the sacred.'[20] In a perceptive essay, Thomas M. Greene has noticed that Jonson's 'intuition of the centered self continued to leave room for an exuberant if discriminating curiosity. The compass, keeping still one foot upon its center, never ceased to swing its other foot wide in firm and unwearied arcs.'[21] This appears very well to describe the play of wit in Jonson's non-dramatic verse, at once given scope by the poet's stance and controlled (so to speak) by a 'larger' conception of decorum than that which is to the fore in the plays.

The common or garden sense of the term 'decorum' is 'that which is proper, suitable, seemly, befitting, becoming; fitness, propriety, congruity ... *esp.* in dramatic, literary, or artistic composition. ... that which is proper

to a personage, place, time, or subject in question' (OED).
Thus, Jonson observes that 'Sidney did not keep a
Decorum in making every one speak as well as himself,'
and that 'Guarini in his Pastor Fido kept not decorum in
making shepherds speek as well as himself could.'[22] The
plays, of course, as Barish points out, everywhere reflect
Jonson's 'especially acute concern for decorum, the law
which demands that a character speak like himself at all
times.'[23] The playwright, however, who typically expresses 'the modest anger of a *satyricke* spirit,' draws
attention not so much to decorous language and conduct
as to their opposites, the indecorous expressions and
actions of those who 'run wrong.' Barish shows that
Jonson may simply insinuate 'through the texture of the
language, that all is false,' but that ordinarily he inter-
mingles 'the "true" and the "natural" in his character's
speech with the unnaturally appropriated expressions,
the forms of wantonness.'[24] In the plays, in fact, where
Jonson's stance is essentially that of the satirical poet, it
appears that the force of decorum is conveyed in dualistic
terms, by means of oppositions between the appropriate
and the inappropriate, the noble and the grotesque, the
harmonious and the discordant. And it is regularly the
indecorous language or action, aptly enough for Jonson's
purpose in this medium, that entertains or excites the
auditor, who is thereby (presumably) drawn on to per-
ceive the degree to which his own 'powers of wit, and
soule' may have been perverted or quite neglected.

But the *idea* of decorum, as these remarks imply, moves
in a somewhat larger context than that so far taken
directly under consideration. Edward Partridge, having
dealt with Jonson's attention in the plays to 'the disparity between expectation and fulfillment, appearance
and reality, words and deeds,' adds a warning:

We may lack Jonson's strong sense of decorum, perhaps

135

because we can not entirely agree with his concept of what is natural. Jonson clearly anticipated that sense of 'nature' which became a central dogma in the neo-classic age: that is, the natural is the normal and the universal.[25]

Puttenham's account of the 'good grace of every thing in his kind' is to the point here. Having equated 'decorum' with 'decencie,' 'seemelynesse,' and 'comelynesse,' he continues as follows:

This lovely conformitie, or proportion, or conveniencie betweene the sence and the sensible hath nature her selfe first most carefully observed in all her owne workes, then also by kinde graft it in the appetites of every creature working by intelligence to covet and desire: and in their actions to imitate & performe: and of man chiefly before any other creature aswell in his speaches as in every other part of his behaviour ...[26]

To return for a moment to the OED, 'decorum' may signify 'beauty arising from fitness, or from absence of the incongruous,' and (in particular) 'orderly condition, orderliness,' for which a citation is given from the early seventeenth-century translation by John Healey of *The City of God*: '[The Creator's] wisedome reacheth from end to end, ordering all in a delicate decorum.' To employ the term in these senses is to attend not merely to man's social role, but to his place in nature and his use of time. The term, in fact, implies a philosophical ideal of harmonious order within which the artist employs decorum as a rhetorical tool of consistency; perhaps one may say that the ideal stands to the tool as principle to practice, final to efficient cause.[27]

This 'larger' concept of decorum is implicit in Jonson's allusions to Sidney and Guarini; and it sounds through the description of Donne's 'First Anniversary' as 'profane and full of blasphemies.' Decorum so conceived provides the rationale for the Senecan dictum, 'He that can order him selfe to the Law of nature, is not onely without the sense, but the feare of poverty,' and for that other passage in praise of variety which Jonson drew from Quintilian: 'howsoever wee doe many things, yet are wee (in a sort) still fresh to what wee begin: wee are recreated with change, as the stomacke is with meats.'[28] All men, Jonson would say, can profit by these advices; but for the true poet and critic, who is himself the reflection and exemplar of the full range of a larger order of things, they have a special application.

The order of Gods creatures in themselves, is not only admirable, and glorious, but eloquent; Then he who could apprehend the consequence of things in their truth, and utter his apprehensions as truly, were the best Writer, or Speaker.[29]

And *'Language,'* after all,

springs out of the most retired, and inmost parts of us, and is the Image of the Parent of it, the mind. ... Nay, it is likened to a man; and as we consider feature, and composition in a man; so words in Language: in the greatnesse, aptnesse, sound, structure, and harmony of it.[30]

When the poet, then, puts by 'the modest anger of a *satyricke* spirit,' appropriate to the dramatic medium, in favour of that 'perfect and divine temper' which 'contaynes as much, as man in fulnesse may,' on view chiefly in the non-dramatic verse, his work certainly continues to reflect a controlling law of decorum; but the mode undergoes some alteration. While juxtaposed oppositions of decorous and indecorous elements are still present, Jonson prefers to demonstrate the full range and variety of that which is decorous and appropriate. And the scale (so to speak) has been enlarged. An ignorant public may very probably expect a volume of *Epigrammes* by Ben

Jonson to be 'bold, licentious, full of gall, / Wormwood, and sulphure, sharpe, and tooth'd withall'; yet the poet's primary care appears in the dedication, which observes that the Earl of Pembroke is to lead forth *so many good, and great names (as my verses mention on the better part) to their remembrance with posteritie.*[31]

It is tempting to identify Jonson's wit with his sensitivity to the demands of decorum; but that will not altogether serve. In what, precisely, the wit of Jonson's poetry may be said to consist remains, of course, a somewhat vexed question. George Williamson singles out Jonson's typically antithetical management of the heroic couplet as the operative factor; Wesley Trimpi prefers to emphasize that socially appropriate urbanity of the plain style which reflects Jonson's intellectual sophistication. In the context of Jonson's classicism, Parfitt draws attention to the combined influence on his verse of the English plain-style tradition and the weight, clarity, and exactness of Latin poetry; Spanos speaks rather of 'motion in stillness,' the generation of resonance in the formal construct.[32] Each critic makes a persuasive case. For the purposes of this paper, however, the position taken up by Geoffrey Walton would seem to be especially relevant. Opposing the 'spiritual and intellectual poise' of metaphysical wit to the 'social poise' of Restoration wit, Walton places the wit of Jonson's poetry between these schools, noting on the one hand the poet's 'intellectual discipline and precision' and on the other his 'scrupulous and lively sense of values' as the distinctive marks of his wit.[33] This is very sensible; yet the 'lively' aspect of Jonson's wit is clearly overmatched by those emphases on the disciplined and the scrupulous. No doubt Jonson's wit continues to imply earlier meanings of the term (i.e., 'intellect,' 'mental capacity,' 'mind'); and it also reflects that 'natural Advantage' of Jonson's character identified by Clarendon as 'Judgment to order and govern Fancy, rather than Excess of Fancy.'[34] Still, making every allowance for Jonson's regular insistence on the importance of reasoned judgment, and for the related fact that he is clearly partial to antithetical measures in verse, the wit of Jonson's poetry continues to be informed by a deeply imaginative and very Elizabethan pleasure in the perception of resemblance and analogy. This is not to say that Jonson's poetry typically illustrates what Bacon glumly terms 'the peculiar and perpetual error of the human intellect, [namely] to be more moved and excited by affirmatives than negatives.' It is rather that the perception of similarities (which Bacon associates with the imagination) is for Jonson a source of pleasure at least as rewarding as that derived from 'discerning suddenly *dissimilitudes* in things that otherwise appear the same.'[35] I would not argue that the wit of Jonson's poetry altogether and in detail anticipates the proposition advanced by Hobbes, in 1640, to the effect that wit comprehends both fancy, which perceives similarities, and judgment, which perceives dissimilarities. Yet (to compress Hobbes' language somewhat) his account of 'that *quick ranging* ... virtue of the mind,' which is at once a source of delight and the means by which men 'attain to exact and perfect knowledge,' might very well serve for a basic working definition of Jonson's wit, since it makes room for the liveliness and freedom by which (together with disciplined control) that wit is distinguished.[36] And it seems that if the poet's characteristic stance in the nondramatic verse largely accounts for the free and varied play of Jonson's wit, his attention to a 'larger' decorum, i.e., his concern for 'the consequence of things in their truth,' flexibly controls and conditions that wit.

Jonson knew that the poet must not be 'every where witty ... nothing is more foolish.'[37] The more discerning among his peers emphasize, together with the capacity and range of his wit (as Herrick remarks 'the store' of

'Thy wits great over-plus'), the arch-poet's nice control of it. Here is William Cartwright, for one:

> *Nor dost* thou *poure out, but dispence* thy *veine,*
> *Skill'd when to spare, and when to entertaine:*
> *Not like our* wits, *who into one piece do*
> *Throw all that they can say, and their* friends *too* ...
> ['*In the memory of the most Worthy*
>   Benjamin Johnson,' ll. 59–62]

Carew, alluding to 'the Tapers thriftie waste, / That sleekes thy terser Poems' ('To Ben. Johnson. ...,' 37–8), may glance at this aspect of Jonson's wit; Sidney Godolphin certainly does. For 'little Syd,' Jonson was 'the most *proportion'd Witt,* / To Nature, the *best Judge* of what was fit' ('On Ben Jonson,' ll. 3–4). Yet Jonson himself must have the last word. Having spoken, in a passage drawn from Vives, of the contributions made by arts 'that serve the body' to those 'that respect the mind,' he continues in his own voice:

There is a more secret Cause: *and the power of liberall studies lyes more hid, then that it can bee wrought out by profane wits. It is not every mans way to hit. They are men (I confesse) that set the* Caract, *and* Value *upon things, as they love them; but* Science *is not every mans* Mistresse. *It is as great a spite to be praised in the wrong place, and by a wrong person, as can be done to a noble nature.*[88]

What does Jonson intend by that intriguing expression, 'a more secret *Cause*'? An earlier passage from *Timber* is helpful in this regard. 'In being able to counsell others,' Jonson observes,

a Man must be furnish'd with an universall store in him-selfe, to the knowledge of all Nature: *That is the matter, and seed-plot; There are the seats of all* Argument, *and*

Invention. But especially, you must be cunning in the
nature of Man: There is the variety of things, which are
as the Elements, *and* Letters, *which his art and wisdom*
must ranke, and order to the present occasion.[39]

The 'more secret *Cause,*' then, presumably refers to the
capacity of the individual (notably the true poet and
critic) to recognize and express every aspect of the varied
order that informs nature; and to respond, by a wit at
once 'quick ranging' and decorously restrained, to that
larger 'principle of dynamic unity.' Further, that the poet
derives keen pleasure from the exercise of his wit requires
some emphasis: one can, perhaps, make too much of the
plain style, the concern for ethical values, the 'sage and
serious' element in Jonson's work. The Jonson whose
'Jeasts and Apothegms' Drummond so fortunately
thought to record ought not altogether to be neglected:
this poet can praise 'a noble, and right generous mind /
(To vertuous moods inclin'd)' and yet savour 'the good
Pleasure of Muscadel and eggs.'[40] The variety of his wit,
ranging decorously from the gamesome and the sprightly
to the higher reaches of what T.S. Eliot has called 'holy
mirth,'[41] reflects the poet's full delight in his craft.

While it is chiefly the longer and more substantial
poems that may be thought to represent at full the wit of
Jonson's non-dramatic verse, it is instructive to notice,
first, the variously witty character of one or two slighter
pieces; then to consider the somewhat larger scope of
groups or clusters of poems addressed to the same person,
or centred on a common theme. Throughout, as one
moves from relatively simple to rather more complex
forms, the attention to decorum that governs Jonson's
pleasing wit renders it regularly compatible with that
high seriousness typical of the poet who can 'apprehend
the consequence of things in their truth, and utter his
apprehensions as truly.'

I should like to glance first at two shorter poems among the *Epigrammes* which have not attracted much critical attention but which are interestingly relevant.[42]

XL. ON MARGARET RATCLIFFE

M arble, weepe, for thou dost cover
A dead beautie under-neath thee,
R ich, as nature could bequeath thee:
G rant then, no rude hand remove her.
A ll the gazers on the skies
R ead not in faire heavens storie,
E xpresser truth, or truer glorie,
T hen they might in her bright eyes.
R are, as wonder, was her wit;
A nd like Nectar ever flowing:
T ill time, strong by her bestowing,
C onquer'd hath both life and it.
L ife, whose griefe was out of fashion,
I n these times. Few so have ru'de
F ate, in a brother. To conclude,
F or wit, feature, and true passion,
E arth, thou hast not such another.

At first blush, the acrostical epitaph for Margaret Ratcliffe (especially in the light of Jonson's deprecating allusion, in the 'Execration Upon Vulcan,' to '*Acrostichs*, and *Telestichs*, on jumpe names') would not appear to be notably decorous in itself or in its context of poems described by their author as '*the ripest of* [his] *studies*.' Admittedly, too, the epitaphs in memory of the poet's first daughter and first son are cast in another mould. One ought to notice, however, the dry observation that Margaret's grief for her brother 'was out of fashion, / In these times.' The acrostical mode of this epitaph, then, is in one sense ironically appropriate to the trivial and selfish character of that society within which Margaret lived, mourned, and died. Yet the decorous contexts of the poem are chiefly positive. While an epitaph marks the death of a mortal creature, it also, typically, gives expression to a pleasing vision of immortal life. So Jonson imagines his Mary among the 'virgin-traine' of 'heavens Queene,' while his first son, having 'scaped worlds, and fleshes rage,' has been safely returned to the bosom of the divine Lender. These innocents are assigned appropriately passive roles in the poems that commemorate them; somewhat similarly, the epitaph for Salomon Pavy has the air of a charming folk-tale,[43] suited in its gentle rallying humour to the years and experience of the youthful actor whom Heaven has vowed to keep. As for Margaret Ratcliffe, a maid of honour at the court of Elizabeth, it is particularly her wit that Jonson singles out for attention: 'Rare, as wonder, was her wit; / And like *Nectar* ever flowing.' Accordingly, the poem opens with the demand for a miracle: 'Marble, weepe ...'; thenceforward, from the letters of Margaret's name, incised in the stone, progressively (and wittily) flow those qualities which made her what she was in life, notably that very wit which enabled time at last to triumph. In short, the poem is thrice decorous: ironically, in a social context; but more seriously, by virtue both of its genre (which permits the poet to confer on inert marble a capacity for lively expression) and of Margaret's character, which demands an appropriately witty memorial. Gamesome, even contrived, the poem may well be; nor would one call it a 'finished' piece. But any hint of the superficial that may initially be implied by the poem's form is surely cancelled by the quiet simplicity of language and syntax, so delicately appropriate for this form and its occasion. The pervasive tone of the poem aptly reflects Jonson's care for that '*Discretio*' which includes 'Respect to discerne, what fits your selfe; him to whom you write; and that which you handle, which is a quality fit to conclude the rest, because it does include all.'[44]

Epigram xci, 'To Sir Horace Vere,' is variously decorous in a way that begins to hint at larger principles of orderliness in the artist's universe.

Which of thy names I take, not onely beares
 A romane *sound, but* romane *vertue weares,*
Illustrous Vere, *or* Horace; *fit to be*
 Sung by a Horace, *or a* Muse *as free;*
Which thou art to thy selfe: whose fame was wonne
 In th'eye of Europe, *where thy deeds were done,*
When on thy trumpet shee did sound a blast,
 Whose rellish to eternitie shall last.
I leave thy acts, which should I prosequute
 Throughout, might flatt'rie seeme; and to be mute
To any one, were envie: which would live
 Against my grave, and time could not forgive.
I speake thy other graces, not lesse showne,
 Nor lesse in practice; but lesse mark'd, lesse knowne:
Humanitie, and pietie, which are
 As noble in great chiefes, as they are rare.
And best become the valiant man to weare,
 Who more should seeke mens reverence, then feare.

The account given by Thomas Fuller of this distinguished soldier and his brother Sir Francis, also a military man, is relevant: Fuller remarks Sir Horace Vere's 'excellent temper, it being true of him what is said of the Caspian Sea, that it doth never ebb nor flow: observing a constant tenor, neither elated nor depressed with success.' Comparing the brothers, Fuller observes, 'Sir Francis was more feared, Sir Horace more loved, by the soldiers.'[45] The first eight lines of Jonson's poem draw attention chiefly to Vere's active and soldierly qualities; by repeating the term *'romane,'* Jonson invites the reader to attend primarily to the Latin signification of Vere's name, and so to recognize that Sir Horace, in the first instance, makes one of those 'true souldiers' addressed

in Epigram CVIII. The association of arms and letters
noticed in lines 3–4 is of course also entirely in keeping
with the ancient tradition that 'Poetry is the companion
of the camps.'[46] The allusion to 'a *Muse* as free,' however, within the compass of lines extolling Vere's active
soldiership, reinforces the hinted ambivalence of 'Which
of thy names I take,' and subtly prepares for the concluding emphasis on those 'other graces' that one does
not ordinarily or at once associate with warlike figures,
the 'humanitie, and pietie' especially becoming to 'the
valiant man,' the complete *vir*. Sir Horace, then, stands
as an emblem of mutually supportive action and knowledge, the one expressed by sounding brass, the other by
quiet and seemly attire. The witty word-play of the
poem's opening has provided guide-lines, so to speak,
for a portrait epitomizing the various wealth of man's
nature. Nor is the creator of this splendidly decorous
poem absent. It is altogether appropriate to the poem's
conception, no doubt, that having spoken of Vere in
terms of 'eternitie,' the poet should emphasize his own
place within the scope and control of time. Yet he does,
after all, position himself at the very centre of the poem
he has created, as if to confirm the artist's joy in his
work: 'Ben Jonson made me.'

Professor Spanos has drawn attention to Jonson's
Epigram LXXVI as an instance of 'distorting a conventional form' (i.e., composing a poem based on but not
precisely reproducing the form of the English sonnet),
in the larger cause of 'generating resonance in the well-
wrought formal construct.' I think that he is right about
this; but I think too that the poem takes its place, within
a larger frame of reference, as one in a triad of pieces
addressed to the Countess of Bedford, each of which is
set out in terms appropriate to a particular aspect of her
being: three ways of looking at a Countess, one might
say. It seems also to be true that in each epigram the

place and role assumed by the poet are decorously ad-
justed to match the controlling modes of the several
poems.

LXXXIV. TO LUCY COUNTESSE OF BEDFORD

Madame, *I told you late how I repented,*
I ask'd a lord a buck, and he denyed me;
And, ere I could aske you, I was prevented:
For your most noble offer had supply'd me.
Straight went I home; and there most like a Poet,
I fancied to my selfe, what wine, what wit
I would have spent: how every Muse *should know it,*
And Phoebus-*selfe should be at eating it.*
O Madame, *if your grant did thus transferre mee,*
Make it your gift. See whither that will beare mee.

Epigram LXXXIV, the least of the three, is a rather jolly
affair: essentially anecdotal, familiar, even playful in
tone, its feminine rhymes and conversational manner
draw attention primarily to the easy grace with which
the Countess discharges her social obligations. The poem
may usefully be associated with Jonson's celebration, in
'To Penshurst,' of that truly aristocratic hospitality which
underscores the real presence of social community; and
also, negatively, with Jonson's experience at 'my Lord
Salisburie's table.' In these circumstances, it is proper
that the poet, who in fancy entertains each Muse and the
god of wit beside, should adopt the jovial style of address
in which the witty legalisms of the poem's conclusion are
couched. For the Countess is 'noble'; she not only keeps,
but is herself an emblem of 'holy lawes / Of nature, and
societie.'[47]

LXXVI. ON LUCY COUNTESSE OF BEDFORD

This morning, timely rapt with holy fire,
I thought to forme unto my zealous Muse,
What kinde of creature I could most desire,
To honor, serve, and love; as Poets *use.*

146

I meant to make her faire, and free, and wise,
  Of greatest bloud, and yet more good than great;
I meant the day-starre should not brighter rise,
  Nor lend like influence from his lucent seat.
I meant shee should be curteous, facile, sweet,
  Hating that solemne vice of greatnesse, pride;
I meant each softest vertue, there should meet,
  Fit in that softer bosome to reside.
Onely a learned, and a manly soule
  I purpos'd her; that should, with even powers,
The rock, the spindle, and the sheeres controule
  Of destinie, and spin her owne free houres.
Such when I meant to faine, and wish'd to see,
  My Muse *bad,* Bedford *write, and that was shee.*

If Epigram LXXXIV is chiefly social in bearing, Epigram
LXXVI adopts a more precisely ethical emphasis: Jonson
does not neglect the Countess of Bedford's role as pro-
tectress of poets, but his primary concern is to call the
roster of her virtues. The order and arrangement of these
are of some interest. Appropriately, those to which honour is most apparently due – beauty, wisdom, gentility –
are linked to this lady's bright influence; a tribute follows to the subtler and more 'inward' power of true
courtesy to baffle vice, a power that needs must stir responsive love in the understanding witness. At length,
it is the soul's power to control and even in some sense
'make' one's allotted portion of time that mildly enforces
Jonson's willing service. That the Countess, finally,
should 'spin her owne free houres' aptly recalls those
virtues with which the poet began his account; more to
the point, the expression imparts life and motion to the
finished portrait, 'So lively and so like' (Jonson invites
the thoughtful reader to murmur) 'that living sence it
fayled.' It may be that the poem's shape indicates (besides the 'resonance' suggested by Spanos) its author's

care for matters other than the merely courtly or social, as Jonson reproduces the sonnet form only to press beyond its limits. Certainly the portrait of Lucy represents a figure in society, perhaps, but scarcely of it; her brightness equals that of the day-star, she controls her own destiny. Still, she is explicitly a 'creature'; and it is to the meeting in her nature of every virtue that the reader's attention is chiefly directed, as (in 'Epode') Jonson extols 'A body so harmoniously compos'd, / As if *Nature* disclos'd / All her best symmetrie in that one feature!' If Donne's 'Anniversary' described 'the Idea of a Woman and not as she was,' Jonson's poem, while it has something in common with the other, manages to keep in view the actual Countess of Bedford, on whose courteous generosity a poet may rely. It is the more appropriate that this poet (who has 'an exact knowledge of all virtues') should make a place for himself in the scene: not, to be sure, carousing with Phoebus and the Muses at the festive board, but quietly collaborating with a single 'zealous *Muse*,' introducing and, as it were, 'signing' the portrait they have together made.

XCIV. TO LUCY, COUNTESSE OF BEDFORD, WITH MR DONNES SATYRES

Lucy, *you brightnesse of our spheare, who are*
 Life of the Muses *day, their morning-starre!*
If workes (not th'authors) their owne grace should
  looke,
 Whose poems would not wish to be your booke?
But these, desir'd by you, the makers ends
 Crowne with their owne. Rare poemes aske rare
  friends.
Yet, Satyres, *since the most of mankind bee*
 Their un-avoided subject, fewest see:
For none ere tooke that pleasure in sinnes sense,
 But, when they heard it tax'd, tooke more offence.

They, then, that living where the matter is bred,
* Dare for these poemes, yet, both aske, and read,*
And like them too; must needfully, though few,
* Be of the best: and 'mongst those, best are you.*
Lucy, *you brightnesse of our spheare, who are*
* The* Muses *evening, as their morning-starre.*

With Epigram XCIV, finally, the case is once more, and
profoundly, altered. Lucy's brightness, not merely
matched with that of the day-star, is itself that of the
'morning-starre,' and indeed the source of light and life
for 'our spheare,' with all that it contains, notably the
making of poetry. If the central emphasis of Epigram
LXXXIV is social, and that of Epigram LXXVI ethical, this
poem may perhaps be termed metaphysical in tone. Its
occasion remains in view, of course: that the Countess
should 'dare' to read Donne's *Satyres* (and 'like them
too') glances once more at her virtue. But the total effect
of the poem is keyed to that opening allusion to 'our
spheare.' A power more than natural descends to this
sin-worn mould, touches and by implication transmutes
evil, then mildly resumes its high and heavenly station,
whence its constant beam lightens the darkness and
brings the dawn. This circular movement is precisely
matched by the poem's language and imagery: the former,
plain to a fault, touches on '*Satyres*' and 'sinnes sense'
only at the centre of the poem; as for images, aside from
the controlling figure with which the poem begins and
ends, they are effectively muted, that the vital lamp which
is Lucy shall cast its beam uninterruptedly over the poem.
And, with perfect tact, Jonson absents himself altogether,
save 'as a disembodied voice.' These are the highest
reaches of verse-compliment; yet one perceives the poet's
art largely by virtue of those other tributes to the lady.
As 'E.K.' has it,

all as in most exquisite pictures they use to blaze and portraict not onely the daintie lineaments of beautye, but also rounde about it to shadow the rude thickets and craggy clifts, that by the basenesse of such parts, more excellency may accrew to the principall. ...[48]

In these three poems, then, severally decorous in their kind, is wittily reflected a sector of the order of 'things in their truth'; and Jonson has taken care, now overtly, now by ways less direct, that his readers may, if they will, recognize this poet's capacity to 'apprehend and utter' that order.

The three poems addressed to Mary, Lady Wroth, might equally be instanced in this regard. In the playful sonnet (*The Under-wood*, XXVIII) which attends primarily to Lady Mary's social role within a courtly milieu, the concluding sestet draws a graceful analogy between her verses, '*Cupids* Armorie,' and the girdle of Venus. In Epigram CV, however, the context is more than merely social or courtly; she is imagined as '*Natures Index*,' who can restore the lost treasures of 'all antiquitie'; the mythological imagery of this poem, accordingly, is almost riotously elaborate, to bring home the rich wealth of her character. The mode of Epigram CIII, finally, is quite different in kind: Lady Mary is 'a *Sydney*,'

> *And, being nam'd, how little doth that name*
> *Need any* Muses *praise to give it fame?*

She is, simply, an image of heroic virtue; to recognize that is to dispense altogether with decorative helps. So Jonson points the moral in language that is spare and severe:

> *My praise is plaine, and where so ere profest,*
> *Becomes none more than you, who need it least.*

The two poems addressed to Elizabeth, Countess of

Rutland, are also to the point. Both pieces celebrate that lady's heroic virtue; but where the 'Epistle' (*The Forrest*, xII), conceived in relatively extensive social and historical terms, weaves about the Countess an elaborate pattern of images drawn from heroic legend, the wit of Epigram LXXIX consists chiefly in the taut and challenging logic by which Jonson manages to celebrate Sir Philip Sidney's genius equally with his daughter's 'rare, and absolute' quality. Further, as with the pieces directed to the Countess of Bedford, the poet is decorous too: in the expansive 'Epistle,' one may properly make large claims, to match the deeds of an Orpheus or share the poetic raptures of a Sidney; but the quiet allusion to poets' rarity with which Jonson begins Epigram LXXIX is at once directed explicitly to Sir Philip Sidney, and at last to the Countess of Rutland herself.[49]

It would be interesting and fruitful to take under consideration the full range of those non-dramatic poems in which Jonson deals with love, notwithstanding the disclaimer with which *The Forrest* opens. Wesley Trimpi, to be sure, has an enlightening essay on just this topic; his analysis of 'A Celebration of Charis,' I dare say, may reasonably be called definitive. Still, his emphasis on the plain style leaves room for some discussion of the poet's wit in those pieces, within the context of a larger decorum. One might, for instance, relate the varying metrical effects and the employment of imagery to the central emphases of those lyrics in *The Under-wood* that reflect 'wavering wemens wit,' or to the 'metaphysical' variety of the 'Elegies.' There is room too for an extended analysis in this regard of the poems that deal with the nature and the claims of friendship. So large an undertaking cannot be in place here. But I should like to conclude this paper with some remarks on a poem that has received very little attention, the 'Epithalamion' on the nuptials of Jerome Weston and Frances Stuart, and another piece that most critics have admired, the Pindaric ode on 'that noble paire, Sir Lucius Cary, and Sir H. Morison.' I do not pretend that these poems are equally successful; but each has a peculiar relevance to the matters with which this paper has been concerned.

What chiefly matters about the 'Epithalamion,' perhaps, is that one should not allow oneself to be dazzled by the achievements of Spenser and Herrick in this kind. It is certainly in some degree true to say, as Trimpi rather impatiently does say, that 'the long "Epithalamion" for the marriage of Jerome Weston resembles a royal progress which accidentally happened to take place in a chapel; Charles and his retinue are given considerably more attention than the nuptial pair.'[50] But Jonson's tactfully sparing allusions to the 'longing Couple' and their anticipations of 'a Feast behind' have not much in common with those heated fancies that enliven the elaborate tapestry of Herrick's 'Nuptiall Song ... on Sir Clipseby Crew and his Lady'; nor is Jonson's poem composed in quite the same context of Christian humanism that provides the shaping dimensions for Spenser's 'Epithalamion,' although it does surely in some ways reflect the influence of that work. That the high ceremony of Christian marriage has solemn meaning for Jonson is clear enough:

> It is the kindly Season of the time,
>   The Month of youth, which calls all Creatures forth
> To doe their Offices in Natures Chime,
>   And celebrate (perfection at the worth)
>   Mariage, the end of life,
>   That holy strife,
>   And the allowed warre:
> Through which not only we, but all our Species are.

Marriage, then, is holy and entirely natural; but in particular it is timely, not merely in that it is 'seasonable,' but especially in the now obsolete sense of 'keeping time

152

or measure.' The marriage ceremony recalls and collects past time; and also it promises a renewal of 'the large Pedigree' in the time to come. This is an emphasis repeated and elaborated throughout the poem, its application ranging from the assurance of 'a race to fill your Hall' to genial reminders of 'all that elder Lovers know.'

What marks this marriage out from others, however, is the fact of its sponsorship by the royal couple, 'Whose Majesties appeare, / To make more cleare / This Feast, then can the Day'; with 'Crownes, and Kingdomes in their either hand,' Charles and Henrietta Maria, attended by the 'Court, and all the Grandees,' are the truly central figures in this emblematic pageant of social order. 'It is their Grace, and favour, that makes seene, / And wonder'd at, the bounties of this day.' In fact, a Christian and natural orderliness, extending through time, is united with that hierarchical order of English society which draws together at this place, in this moment of time, about 'th'exampled Paire ... Who the whole Act expresse.' It is proper that three stanzas at the heart of the poem should be devoted to the groom's father, Lord Weston; for, as Treasurer of the realm, it is his function to maintain 'just Standard'

> In all the prov'd assayes,
> And legall wayes
> Of Tryals, to worke downe
> Mens Loves unto the Lawes, and Lawes to love the
> Crowne.

That is to say, he directs the energies of man's desires into those socially sanctioned channels that help to preserve the ordered community of men, and, perhaps chiefly, to perpetuate its quality.

The poem is designed to throw just these matters into high relief. To observe that it is made up of twenty-four stanzas, and that their metrical pattern is (for Jonson) relatively complex, is of course to think of Spenser's example; but Jonson's debt to his grand predecessor is only of the most general kind. Evidently he endorsed the decorous matching of elaborate verse-form to ceremoniously formal occasion; and his employment of the alexandrine follows that of Spenser. It may also be that he thought it fitting to celebrate in just twenty-four stanzas a theme and personages that might be termed in some sense heroic. 'Th'exampled Paire,' after all, are 'the mirrour of their kind.' But the structure of Jonson's poem does not reproduce that exquisitely modulated arrangement of light and sound imagery that accompanies the progressive movement of Spenser's marriage ode. Specifically, the sun is not permitted to trace its smooth arc in the heavens above the events taking place at Roehampton; instead, having been induced by the poet to arrest its course, the sun is drawn into conversation, made to admire the bride, the procession, the royal pair, and at length sent posting away: in the first instance, to complete its rounds, but chiefly (as 'officious Sun') to hasten on the consummation of these nuptials. The effects of this manoeuvre are several. Initially, speaker and sun are linked as relatively simple lookers-on at the gorgeous spectacle that is toward; in consequence, as the poem proceeds, the suggestion that 'all [the sun's] age of Journals' was directed to this place, this brilliantly social occasion, is the more persuasive; at last, the sun is itself enlisted in the ceremony, and, imaginatively, made one of the officious retinue attending on the royal couple.

This emphasis on the interplay of temporal and social order is reinforced by Jonson's management of imagery. Within its Christian frame of reference, classical and conventionally metaphysical images are alike repudiated: 'Force from the Phoenix, then, no raritie / Of Sex, to rob the Creature ...'; nor 'dare [we] aske our wish in Language *fescennine*.' Nothing, to be sure, can 'Illustrate' the monarch and his consort, to whom the poet has early directed our gaze, 'but they / Themselves today, / Who the whole Act expresse.' Yet for the rest, the imagery of social converse is most proper: '*Caroches*' all the way from Greenwich to Roehampton, then, bring together 'Our Court, and all the Grandees,' headed by the 'Great Say-Master of State'; while the bridegroom himself is identified, at last, as 'Master of the Office.' And the poet, having sent the sun about his business, stands forth to point the moral of all that has occurred:

> *Th'Ignoble never liv'd, they were a-while*
>   *Like Swine, or other Cattell here on earth:*
> *Their names are not recorded on the File*
>   *Of Life, that fall so ...*

But the 'noble Nature,' that speaks through 'a reaching Vertue, early and late,' keeps up posterity and bestows a lasting impress upon time, which has value by virtue of man's ordered use of it, epitomized in the Christian and social gathering at Roehampton.

It is in the ode to Cary and Morison, however, that Jonson most wittily displays his command of variously decorous expression, together with (or better, united to) his own delight in the creative act by which that mastery is demonstrated.[51] The 'Epithalamion' celebrated a cheerful occasion: Jonson therefore required principally to select particular aspects of that occasion, and, by judicious placement and emphasis, establish its symbolic relevance in the stream of time. In a sense, the thing was almost too easy, the challenge insufficient. As the poet steps before his audience to provide a gloss, one may feel that, for all its art, the poem has a certain rough-cast about it. By contrast, untimely death provides the occasion for Jonson's ode; the poet, initially gloomy and dejected, must find his own way up to light through and by means of the process of composition itself. The truth of that obser-

155

vation in *Timber,* 'Language ... springs out of the most retired, and inmost parts of us, and is the Image of the Parent of it, the mind,' is dis-covered and demonstrated, one might say, in the progressively more witty analogies and correspondences of the ode. There is no need for the artist to point out the 'meaning' of his work; this poem, at last, points to itself.

Classical legend provides Jonson with an example appropriate to the mood of gloomy disenchantment that pervades the first two stanzas of the poem: chiefly in evidence are darkness, death, and 'utmost ruine,' paired with the element of fire. For thoughtful readers, however, the primary emphasis is that of incompleteness:

> *... could they but lifes miseries fore-see,*
> *No doubt all Infants would returne like thee?*

Yet the fact that the thought is put as a question indicates the essentially tentative nature of these sombre musings; the contradictory association, too, of 'wiser Nature' with negative and abortive action indicates that these initial hypotheses are unsatisfactory, although the structural pattern of the poem (mirroring the progress of its author's thought) has at least been established:

> *How summ'd a circle didst thou leave man-kind*
> *Of deepest lore, could we the Center find!*

By thoughtful attention to particular events or persons to draw out, through analogy and correspondence, the full implications of man's destiny: that is the poet's task.

The lines that immediately follow are subtly framed. Logically, they continue and extend to present experience the dismal emphases of the opening stanzas; nevertheless, by the movement from legend to 'fact,' a step has been taken toward the apprehension of 'real' truth. Further, although the account given of one who 'vexed time, and ... Troubled both foes, and friends; / But ever to no ends,' continues the earlier emphasis on incompleteness, the figures by which Jonson traces this 'Stirrer's' career make play, no longer with fire, but with air and water. The 'flight,' such as it is, concludes ignominiously in 'that dead sea of life'; still, at least a half-life remains. 'The Corke of Title boy'd him up,' Jonson observes, with an ironic smile.

Just here, and perhaps in response to that wryly amusing figure, the poem alters in emphasis; one would say, 'changes direction,' but for the fact that the pattern of analogy and correspondence is so smoothly maintained. Having glanced at the anonymous ancient whose sordid career cancelled an early promise, Jonson now turns his gaze directly on Morison, who, cut off in youth, much more than 'summ'd a circle'; 'His life was of Humanitie the Spheare.' What is especially remarkable about this part of the poem is Jonson's metaphorical association of life and art, which begins with the cheerful reminder that Morison 'never fell, thou fall'st, my tongue,' continues in the account of Morison's career as 'ample, full, and round, / In weight, in measure, number, sound,' and then, at the very centre of the poem, reaches joyfully on to what one might call Jonson's credo:

> Life doth her great actions spell,
> By what was done and wrought
> In season, and so brought
> To light: her measures are, how well
> Each syllab'e answer'd, and was form'd,
>   how faire;
> These make the lines of life, and that's her
>   ayre.

The chiseled purity of the stanza that follows is justly famous. But one ought not to overlook the fact that the round of elements is completed with those allusions to tree, plant, and 'flowre of light,' for the remainder of the ode makes play with the irradiation of earth by a light at once natural and divine. Light, it may be noted, first appears in the poem virtually at the instant of Jonson's recognition that the disciplined forms of art 'make the lines of life.'

The rest is celebration; and also prophecy. The wine and garlands of classical revelry are quite appropriate for the poet-priest who has thrust beyond legend and fact to the realm of prophetic truth. Morison's 'bright eternall Day' promises as much for all 'happy men'; the friendship that death cannot destroy stands symbol of a larger kinship between heaven and earth ('Whilst that in heav'n, this light on earth must shine'), and also of that community of good men which Jonson so highly values, keyed to the

> *simple love of greatnesse, and of good;*
> *That knits brave minds, and manners, more*
> *than blood.*

And in the midst of the hymns and hallelujahs, someone may be seen turning witty handsprings: Ben Jonson, in fact, with decorous delight in his art, disporting himself between counter-turn and stand as he celebrates the united hearts of 'these twi- / Lights, the *Dioscuri.*' Finally, as the piece draws to a close, the poet, first glancing back at the controlled combination of knowledge and action by which each friend 'grew a portion of the other,' confirms the continuing power of 'the faire example.' As this friendship was made fact in time by 'two so early men,' whose lives symbolically overmastered seasonal change, so mankind may expect at last to triumph over time.

In a famous passage, Milton speaks of 'closing up truth to truth as we find it, (for all her body is homogeneal, and proportional,) this is the golden rule in theology as well as in arithmetic, and makes up the best harmony in a church ...'[52] Jonson also, in his poetry, by the exercise of a wit at once lively and controlled, is in a real sense 'closing up truth to truth.' The epigram to Sir William Jephson might fittingly apply to the poet himself: 'So did thy vertue'enforme, thy wit sustaine / That age, when thou stood'st up the master-braine.' But it is Epigram cxxviii ('To William Roe') that provides the aptest figure for Jonson's conception of the larger responsibility to which the poet and critic must attend:

> th'art now, to goe
> Countries, and climes, manners, and men to know,
> T'extract, and choose the best of all these knowne,
> And those to turne to bloud, and make thine owne:
> May windes as soft as breath of kissing friends,
> Attend thee hence; and there, may all thy ends,
> As the beginnings here, prove purely sweet,
> And perfect in a circle alwayes meet.

NOTES

1 'The Life and Writings of Addison,' in *Literary Essays Contributed to The Edinburgh Review* [1843] (London 1913), 610–11

2 *The Life of John Dryden* [1834], ed. B. Kreissman (Lincoln, Neb. 1963), 227

3 *A Study of Ben Jonson* (London 1889), 95

4 L.C. Knights, *Drama and Society in the Age of Jonson* (London 1937), 185; F.R. Leavis, *Revaluation: Tradition and Development in English Poetry* (London 1936), 10–36; Wesley Trimpi, *Ben Jonson's Poems: A Study of the Plain Style* (Stanford, Cal. 1962); Geoffrey Walton, *From Metaphysical to Augustan: Studies in Tone and Sensibility in the Seventeenth Century* (London 1955); William V. Spanos, 'The Real Toad in the Jonsonian Garden: Resonance in the Nondramatic Poetry,' *JEGP*, LXVIII (1969), 1–23. The quotation is taken from G.A.E. Parfitt, 'The Poetry of Ben Jonson,' *EIC*, XVIII (1968), 18–31.

5 Joseph Summers, *The Muse's Method: An Introduction to Paradise Lost* (Cambridge, Mass. 1962), 21. I am indebted also to the comments on decorum made by Rosemond Tuve, *Elizabethan and Metaphysical Imagery* (Chicago 1961), and by Thomas Kranidas, *The Fierce Equation: A Study of Milton's Decorum* (The Hague 1965).

6 *Ben Jonson*, ed. C.H. Herford, Percy and Evelyn Simpson, 11 vols (Oxford 1925–52), VIII, 595. Citations from Jonson's works refer to the text of this edition, cited hereafter as *H & S*.

7 *H & S*, III, 432 (*EMO*, 'Induction,' 120–2)

8 *H & S*, III, 423 (*EMO*, 'The Character of the Persons,' 1–2); IV, 157–8, 180 (*CR*, v.iv.612,650; xi.137)

9 *H & S*, V, 432 (*Catiline*, 'To the Reader in Ordinairie'); IV, 301 (*Poetaster*, v.iii.144); v, 24 (*Volpone*, 'Prologue,' 29)

10 *H & S*, IV, 301 (*Poetaster*, v.iii.138)

11 *H & S*, VI, 269 (*The Divell is an Asse*, v.viii.172–4)

12 *H & S*, IV, 158 (*CR*, v.iv.644–6)

13 *The Student's Milton*, ed. F.A. Patterson (New York 1945), 549; *H & S*, V, 17 (*Volpone*, 'To ... The Two Famous Universities')

14 *H & S*, IV, 74 (*CR*, II.iii.123–40)

15 *H & S*, V, 17 (*Volpone*, 'To ... The Two Famous Universities')

16 Henry Adams, *The Education of Henry Adams* (New York 1931), 378–90

17 Hugh Maclean, 'Ben Jonson's Poems: Notes on the Ordered Society,' in *Essays in English Literature from the Renaissance to the Victorian Age*, ed. M. MacLure and F.W. Watt (Toronto 1964), 43–68

18 *H & S*, IV, 168 (*CR*, v.viii.19–20)

19 *Laws*, vii.803

20 J. Huizinga, *Homo Ludens: A Study of the Play Element in Culture* (Boston 1950), 19. Cf. also, on [Elizabethan] wit 'as the play of the mind ... an intellectual pleasure,' A. Stein, *John Donne's Lyrics: The Eloquence of Action* (Minneapolis, Minn. 1962), 90.

21 Thomas M. Greene, 'Ben Jonson and the Centered Self,' *SEL*, x (1970), 325–48

22 *H & S*, I, 132, 134

23 Jonas Barish, *Ben Jonson and the Language of Prose Comedy* (Cambridge, Mass. 1960), 92

24 Ibid., 93

25 E.B. Partridge, *The Broken Compass: A Study of the Major Comedies of Ben Jonson* (New York 1958), 171

26 George Puttenham, *The Arte of English Poesie, 1589* (Menston 1968), 219. H.S. Wilson, in 'Some Meanings of "Nature" in Renaissance Literary Theory,' *JHI*, II (1941), 430–48, notes the growing tendency toward the end of the sixteenth century 'to associate the norm of "nature" with "literary decorum." In Puttenham, literary decorum signifies the artist's perception of the fitness, the harmony, and the proportion in things, a criterion which in one aspect amounts simply to the advice to imitate empirical reality. But this criterion also assumes a certain fixed orderliness in the artist's universe, and Nature grants the power to discern it or the taste to enjoy it, not indiscriminately, but only to those of "learned and experienced" discretion, strong in reason and schooled in literary tradition.'

27 Those 'senses' of nature, by Wilson's schema, which are especially relevant in this connection are Sense 1 ('Nature as the universe, the sum of things, their order and operation') and Sense 4 ('Nature as empirical reality, especially the typical character, actions, and passions of men'); also Sense 22 ('proportion, propriety, decorum,' considered as 'an attribute or mode of working' of Nature's 'regulative power manifesting itself in the literary activity of men'). Kranidas speaks of 'this larger decorum' as 'a resonant principle of dynamic unity' (*The Fierce Equation*, 48, 32). Cf. also Joseph Summers on Milton's idea of decorum: 'Decorum concerned the proper relations between the parts and the whole, the propriety of means and ends. The "decorous" in this sense, like our modern "functional," implies that beautiful detail must contribute to or reflect

the whole; but unlike the modern word, Milton's term also implies that harmony is natural to man and that man is more than the sum of his activities' (*The Muse's Method*, 21). Rosemond Tuve, finally, observes that 'the principle of "decorum according to the subject" cannot operate under any other conception of poetic truth than the ancient one that poetry deals with things "in their universal consideration"' (*Elizabethan and Metaphysical Imagery*, 246).

28 H & S, VIII, 605, 619–20
29 Ibid., 628
30 Ibid., 625
31 Ibid., 25–6. The comment on 'To Penshurst' by O.B. Hardison, Jr, is relevant: 'Jonson was no less preoccupied with moral teaching than earlier didactic poets, but he seldom sacrificed the sense of reality for the sake of a moral. Instead he preferred to idealize, and this is the strategy of his elegy on Penshurst. Beyond the clearly delineated historical or "true" setting are hints of pastoral innocence, the golden age, and, perhaps, a suggestion of Eden' (*The Enduring Monument: A Study of the Idea of Praise in Renaissance Literary Theory and Practice* [Chapel Hill, NC 1962], 112.)
32 G.A.E. Parfitt, 'Compromise Classicism: Language and Rhythm in Ben Jonson's Poetry,' *SEL*, XI (1971), 109–24; William Spanos, 'The Real Toad in the Jonsonian Garden: Resonance in the Nondramatic Poetry'
33 Geoffrey Walton, *From Metaphysical to Augustan*, ch. 1
34 Edward Hyde, Earl of Clarendon, *The Life of Edward, Earl of Clarendon ...*, 2 vols (Oxford 1760), I, 24
35 Francis Bacon, *Works*, ed. J. Spedding, R.L. Ellis, and D.D. Heath, 14 vols. (London 1857–74), VIII, 80 (and cf. VI, 258–9); Thomas Hobbes, *The Elements of Law Natural and Politic*, ed. F. Tonnies (New York 1969), 50 [I.x]. Cf. also W.L. Ustick and H.H. Hudson, 'Wit, "Mixt Wit," and the Bee in Amber,' *HLB*, VIII (1935), 103–30.
36 Cf. Hobbes, *Elements of Law Natural and Politic*, 50. I am not suggesting, of course, that the wit of Jonson's poetry effectively illustrates Hobbes' subsequent modification of

his earlier view 'to the extent of excluding Judgment from Wit, which he used almost synonomously with Fancy' (Ustick and Hudson, *ibid.*). It may be remarked also that, to the degree that Jonson's wit partakes of that 'definition and dialectic' with which Earl Miner associates 'the wit of Fancy and the wit of Judgment' in metaphysical poetry, whereas Donne typically challenges and extends the bounds of decorum, Jonson is apt rather to draw back from violations of decorum. Cf. Earl Miner, *The Metaphysical Mode from Donne to Cowley* (Princeton, NJ 1969), 118–58; also G. Williamson, *The Proper Wit of Poetry* (London 1961), 20, and A. Stein, *John Donne's Lyrics*, 88, 90.

37 *H & S*, VIII, 581

38 Ibid., 568

39 Ibid., 565. Wilson's Sense 1 and Sense 4 (cf. n27) are chiefly in question here.

40 Ibid., 112 ('Epode,' 111–12); I, 147

41 T.S. Eliot, 'A Note on Two Odes of Cowley,' in *Seventeenth Century Studies Presented to Sir Herbert Grierson* (Oxford 1938), 235–42. What Kranidas observes of Milton applies also to Jonson: 'Always the unity he idealizes and works toward is that of the richly realized individual in a universe of God's making' (*The Fierce Equation*, 157).

42 'His inventions are smooth and easie,' said Drummond, 'but above all he excelleth in a translation' (*H & S*, I, 151). Professor Spanos and others have noticed Jonson's artful fidelity, in 'To Celia' (*The Forrest*, VI), to his own dictum that the ancients are properly 'Guides, not Commanders.' But the translation of the first in Horace's fourth Book of *Odes* provides an interesting example of the poet's wit. In one sense, Jonson's English faithfully reproduces the effects and emphases of his original. The alliteration of 'parce, precor, precor' (1. 2) is precisely matched by 'pray thee, pray thee spare,' while that of lines 4 and 5, 'sub regno Cinarae. desine, dulcium / mater saeva Cupidinum,' is rendered so as to reproduce an alliterative effect: 'I am not such, as in the Reigne / Of the good *Cynara* I was: Refraine ...' Again, 'iecur' (1. 12), given as 'heart' in the

Loeb version, is unflinchingly rendered as 'liver' by one who felt sure that he 'knew more in Greek and Latin, than all the Poets in England.' And the concluding Horatian emphases on the loved one's hardness of heart together with the changeable flood through which the lover is bound to follow, although Jonson shifts their positioning, retain thereby their full impact in his English. At the same time, however, Jonson takes liberties with the text. 'Mater saeva' is rendered, a little unexpectedly, 'Sower Mother'; the youth and the shrewd energy of the speaker's rival, not much more than noticed in the Latin, are thrust to the fore in Jonson's version: 'For he's both noble, lovely, young, / And for the troubled Clyent fyl's his tongue ...' Most strikingly, the neutral 'femina nec puer' of the Latin becomes 'nor Wench, nor wanton Boy.' In short, an element of bitter acidity, instinct in the speaker's personality and informing his view of life, has been added to the poignancy of the original: the poem has acquired thereby something of an ironic edge. This in turn permits the reader fully to appreciate and savour Jonson's exquisite rendering of the speaker's agony: 'But, why, oh why, my *Ligurine*, / Flow my thin teares, downe these pale cheeks of mine?' The translation, in fact, demonstrating Jonson's capacity to bring a learned integrity to language, together with sensitive awareness of the degree to which one may decorously make free with it, recalls and aptly illustrates Greene's allusion to 'the centered self' that can tolerate 'an exuberant if discriminating curiosity.'

43 This is not to deny that it may well be described also as 'an extravagant and sustained conceit in an otherwise classically conceived poem' (Spanos, 'The Real Toad in the Jonsonian Garden: Resonance in the Nondramatic Poetry').

44 *H & S*, VIII, 633. Cf. also Hardison's comments on 'the element of restraint' which, in the epitaph, traditionally 'controls the development of the positive topics of praise' (*The Enduring Monument*, 124–5).

45 *The Worthies of England*, ed. J. Freeman (London 1952), 180

46 Sir Philip Sidney, *An Apology for Poetry*, ed. G. Shepherd (London 1965), 127

47 'Epistle to Katherine, Lady Aubigny' (*The Forrest*, XIII), 18–19

48 *The Works of Edmund Spenser*, ed. E. Greenlaw, C.G. Osgood, F.M. Padelford, and R. Heffner, 10 vols (Baltimore, Md. 1932–49); *The Minor Poems*, I, 8

49 The contrasting modes of those pieces addressed to other poets are of interest in this connection, especially the two epigrams to Donne. S.M. Wiersma has suggested, in 'Jonson's "To John Donne" ' (*Explicator*, XXV [1966], Item 4), that in Epigram XXIII, Jonson compliments Donne by employing the latter's manner. It may be thought, however, that Epigram XCVI provides a better illustration of Wiersma's point, and even that the earlier poem makes its complimentary effect in quite another way. XXIII is very much in what one takes to be Jonson's usual manner in the genre of brief verse compliment: the lines are regularly end-stopped; caesuras fall, more often than not, in mid-line; the person addressed, identified at once, is as quickly placed within a context traditionally classical. The first four lines seem to promise a detailed assessment of those qualities that combinedly account for Donne's genius. But with the fifth and sixth lines, which acknowledge the measureless character of Donne's mind, something on the order of desperation enters the poem; and, after one wild glance at the huge range of the other man's achievement, Jonson abruptly throws in his hand, implicitly acknowledging that the silken lines and silver hooks of his best manner cannot take the evasive quarry of Donne's peculiar art.

Epigram XCVI might almost take its point of departure from the conclusion of the earlier poem. With a wit at once rueful and gracious, Jonson seems deliberately to attempt Donne's manner, without abandoning the pentameter couplets he prefers to employ in the epigrammatic genre. Thus, run-on lines and the mildly erratic placement of caesuras help to bring about a rhythmic movement

quite in contrast to that of the relatively stately Epigram
XXIII; classical images are banished; the abrupt opening,
too, and the accentual challenge of line 3, certainly suggest Donne's way in poetry, as do the syntactical ambi-
guities of the first and eleventh lines. It is almost as if
Jonson, having been forced in the making of Epigram
XXIII to acknowledge a proper humility, undertakes to
demonstrate, in mode and matter, his comprehension of
that virtue.

50 Trimpi, *Ben Jonson's Poems*, 285

51 For Jonson's debt to Seneca, cf. John E. Hankins, 'Jonson's "Ode on Morison" and Seneca's *Epistulae Morales*,'
MLN, LI (1936), 518–20. Of the several comments by
modern critics, that by Earl Miner is among the most in-
cisive: cf. *The Cavalier Mode from Jonson to Cotton*
(Princeton, NJ 1971), 71–4.

52 *The Student's Milton*, 748

BEN JONSON:
PUBLIC ATTITUDES AND
SOCIAL POETRY

L.C. KNIGHTS

John Hollander, in the introduction to his selection of
Jonson's poems in the Laurel Poetry Series, wrote:

*Considering that they are the work of a literary genius,
Ben Jonson's poems have had a curious critical fate. The
epoch that most intimately responded to their virtues
never singled them out for special praise, while our own
age, so acutely conscious of history, acknowledges their
importance and success and at the same time retains a
fundamentally unsympathetic view towards them, seldom praising without apologizing.*

The useful little volume from which I am quoting appeared in 1961. Since then a good deal has been published
that explains and praises without apologizing, notably
Wesley Trimpi's *Ben Jonson's Poems: A Study of the
Plain Style* (1962), and also various articles, to some of
which I shall refer: and I have the impression that more
of the intelligent young have a genuine and unprompted
interest in Jonson's poems than was the case, say, twenty

years ago, when the plays had long outgrown the 'deadly' reputation that *they* had when T.S. Eliot wrote his well known essay. But it is doubtful whether even yet they have the reputation they deserve. It is true that not many of them are poems that one returns to again and again, as one does to the poetry of Herbert, Blake, and Eliot. But the best of them – a larger number than is sometimes supposed – ought to be a living part of the peopled landscape that those who care at all for poetry carry in their minds: without them an important individual voice, that speaks to us even when we are not actually reading poetry, is missing. To define that voice, or – to change the metaphor again – to say as simply as possible what there is in the poems that is capable of nourishing our minds, not as scholars but simply as men, is the purpose of this paper. This involves the attempt to define a particular social mode of verse-writing; for although Jonson wrote a few intimately personal poems, such as 'To Heaven' or the epitaphs for two of his children, the bulk of his poems, as Hollander and others have recognized, are 'public' in a sense in which, for example, Donne's *Songs and Sonets* are not.

It is perhaps unfortunate that I used the term 'social poetry' in my title, for I am quite unable to define it. Certainly it is not a poetic category, even in the sense that love poetry, elegy, or satire can be said to be different 'kinds.' A wide definition would include an enormous number of poems that are not intimately personal, but that have for subject the life of man in society, whether they are occasioned by particular events (e.g., 'An Horatian Ode,' 'Easter 1916') or have a more general reference (e.g. 'Coriolan').[1] Here I use the term to mean poetry written for a particular, fairly limited, social group, or with that group in mind, which embodies or comments on the values of that group. J.B. Bamborough points out that Jonson's Epigrams belong to a literary 'kind' that he calls familiar and moral; that 'except in length there is little difference between them and his longer "Epistles" '; and that – as others have said too – in the bulk of his poetry Jonson aimed at providing 'an English equivalent of Horace's *sermones* – "conversational poems" or, literally, "talks".'[2] But unlike Coleridge's so-called conversation-pieces Jonson's poems do not tend towards meditation in the imagined presence of one or two intimates: they assume a fairly wide public (if not, like the plays, the public at large) whose shared concerns are reflected in the verse. And this public includes not only fellow professionals and scholars but men and women with an assured and often conspicuous place in the Jacobean-Caroline social order.

To say this is to point to the first of various obstacles in the way of appreciation that must at least be recognized. Both Donne and Jonson – to go no further – were dependent on patronage, Donne at all events until he was safely installed as Dean of St Paul's, and Jonson all his life. And the word 'patronage' at once introduces us to a strange and unfamiliar world. It is a world that those of us who have never taken two steps in what are quaintly called the corridors of power are likely to find in many respects objectionable: not only because of the power-struggles centring on the Court, the ferocity of the greed, the courting of favourites, the conspicuous consumption,[3] but also because of the ways in which good and honourable men, as well as men of genius with a worldly streak, accepted an hierarchical system and found nothing dishonourable in seeking the favour of the great.

To read, for example, Hacket's *Life* of Archbishop Williams (*Scrinia Reserata*) is to enter a world very remote from us – one that Donne and Jonson took for granted, but that it costs some imaginative effort for us to reconstruct in our minds. Describing how Williams solicited Buckingham for the Deanery of Westminster, Hacket says, 'The Deanery to be vacated, had many that longed for it; a fortunate Seat, and near the Court: Like the Office over the King of Persia's Garden at Babylon, which was stored with the most delicious fruit'; and he quotes Pliny: 'He that was trusted with the Garden was the Lord of the Palace.' It is obvious that Williams carefully cultivated the great: and in his attitude towards the common people he sometimes sounds like one of Shakespeare's Patricians in *Coriolanus*. Yet there seems no doubt of his probity and charity, especially to scholars, unfortunate gentlemen, and pensioners – 'so great a Dealer,' says Hacket, 'in the Golden Trade of Mercy.' He obtained an office for Selden, and

in sooth there was never a greater stickler than he to bring Afflicted Ones out of Durance and Misery, when he could effect it by Power and Favour: none that lent their hand more readily to raise up those that were cast down. But if a Gentleman of Mr Selden's merit were under the peril of Vindicative Justice, he would stretch his whole interest, and cast his own Robe, as it were to save him.

It is indeed in some important respects a very remote world, and I cannot attempt to sketch it here. But before we make caustic democratic comments on, for example, Donne's flattery of noble ladies, we should at least reflect that the milieu for poets then, as now, was a very mixed affair. We may well be critical of the way in which men of power and their hangers-on grabbed for the richest pickings in the dish of state, just as we may laugh at the circumstances in which Court masques were performed. But we should also remember that some at least of the aristocracy, even quite close to the Court, had a genuine feeling for literature and a wish to promote it. There is reliable evidence to this effect in Clarendon; Heminge and Condell's dedication of the Shakespeare First Folio 'to the most noble and incomparable pair of brethren,' the Earls of Pembroke and Montgomery – like Jonson's dedication of his *Epigrammes* to Pembroke – does not sound like mere flattery; and, as we shall see, although Jonson admitted that he might 'have praysed, unfortunately [someone] that doth not deserve it,'[4] his poems do suggest a courtly and aristocratic circle that was far from unfavourable to learning and letters.[5] All the same, a hostile critic might say that Donne's and Jonson's verse letters to aristocratic patrons were, in effect if not in title, 'epistles mendicant.' This is a charge that cannot be dealt with until we have looked a little further.

A second obstacle may be dealt with more briefly. John Donne's poetic output forms a unity – by which I do not mean anything so simple as a straight progression or even full coherence of attitude. It is merely that all his poems are recognizably by the same person; to understand them we properly make connexions from one to the other, and his 'social' poems – such as the verse letters – are clearly part of one œuvre. Jonson's works are all 'recognizably by the same person,' but even so there is a division within them. Putting it briefly, the plays express strong negative feelings; they are – often savagely – destructive; they do not merely attack abuses in the light of an accepted norm, they bring in question the ability of the society depicted to formulate and make effective any kind of norm that a decent man would find acceptable. As Jonas Barish puts it, 'Something in Jonson insists on probing until it has exposed a layer of folly in everyone, in everything.'[6] In the non-dramatic verse some of the Epigrams, to be sure, are destructive attacks. But the more 'biting' snippets of satire are not characteristic – as they are certainly not among the best – of the poems as a whole, where acceptance of shared codes in a given social order is integral to the poetry. Putting all this in another way, in reading Donne's social verses we are always looking for flashes of the author of *Songs and Sonets*; in reading Jonson's addresses to friends and patrons we are not disappointed when we fail to find the poet of *Volpone*. Or, rather, we ought not to be disappointed, for I suspect that it is the failure to find the comic and destructive dramatist in the author of *The Forrest* that partly explains a certain under-rating of the poems, which form as it were a separate province in Ben Jonson's empire.

The province, I have already suggested, is a limited one; and, as a final stage in clearing the ground for appreciation, it may be helpful to say, at the risk of obviousness, what the poems do *not* do, what it is no use expecting of them. (It does no harm from time to time to remind ourselves how foolish it is to try to make poets conform to any Act of Uniformity.) Ted Hughes says that his writing of poems was partly a continuation of his earlier pursuit of small animals and birds.

The special kind of excitement, the slightly mesmerized and quite involuntary concentration with which you make out the stirrings of a new poem in your mind, then the outline, the mass and colour and clean final form of it, the unique living reality of it in the midst of the general lifelessness, all that is too familiar to mistake. This is hunting and the poem is a new species of creature, a new specimen of the life outside your own.[7]

I doubt whether that would have been intelligible to Jonson, who, he told Drummond, 'wrote all his first [drafts for poems] in prose, for so his master Camden had learned him.'[8] His poems do not read like the tracking down of an unknown quarry; nor do they spring from what Maritain has called 'a wordless musical stir,' nor from 'a musical phrase ringing insistently in the ears,' at first inchoate and only later taking a precise form, as Nadezhda Mandelstam describes the poetic process in her husband, Osip Mandelstam, and in Akhmatova.[9] There is, then, an obvious contrast between Jonson's poetry and the kind of poetry that we are perhaps most

attuned to today, and that our common critical methods
are designed to deal with. I think here of Valéry's account of the genesis of 'Le Cimetière marin,' of the evidence provided by the recently published facsimile of
T.S. Eliot's drafts for *The Waste Land*, and by the drafts
of some of Yeats's most famous poems that show both
poets in the process of finding – as opposed to simply ex-
pressing – their meanings.[10] With Jonson you cannot use
Eliot's distinction between 'poetic thought' and 'the
thought of the poet.'[11] Wesley Trimpi – to pursue this
point a little – speaks of Jonson's preference for couplets,
as not racking the sense, and his dislike of elaborate
rhyme schemes, quoting 'A Fit of Rime against Rime':[12]

> *Rime, the rack of finest wits,*
> *That expresseth but by fits,*
> > *True Conceipt,*
> *Spoyling Senses of their Treasure,*
> *Cosening Judgement with a measure,*
> > *But false weight.*
> *Wresting words, from their true calling ...*

Jonson, however, was wrong to generalize. George Herbert, for example, sometimes seems to have *discovered*
what he wanted to say by wrestling with intricate stanza
patterns; and in general I think it is true to say that many
poets have found not easily conceptualized meanings in
the process of overcoming 'technical' problems. But the
best of Jonson's poems – even the more directly personal
ones – seem to be the expression of something already
formed: they do not explore the more obscure hinterland
from which thought emerges.[13]

All this, however, is only helpful in a limited prepara-
tory way. The important question is, What values do the
poems embody and help to keep alive? Jonson of course
often defines his values by negatives, not only in the
satiric epigrams but in poems that are not predominantly

satirical. The vices are mostly – as in the plays – some kind of lust, either lust in its ordinary sexual meaning or an inordinate itch to get money or power, or simply to be conspicuous and feel important.

> How blest art thou, canst love the countrey, Wroth,
>   Whether by choice, or fate, or both;
> And, though so neere the citie, and the court,
>   Art tane with neithers vice, nor sport:
> That at great times, art no ambitious guest
>   Of Sheriffes dinner, or Maiors feast.
> Nor com'st to view the better cloth of state;
>   The richer hangings, or crowne-plate;
> Nor throng'st (when masquing is) to have a sight
>   Of the short braverie of the night;
> To view the jewells, stuffes, the paines, the wit
>   There wasted, some not paid for yet!
> ...
> Let this man sweat, and wrangle at the barre,
>   For every price, in every jarre,
> And change possessions, oftner with his breath,
>   Then either money, warre, or death:
> Let him, then hardest sires, more disinherit,
>   And each where boast it as his merit,
> To blow up orphanes, widdowes, and their states;
>   And thinke his power doth equall Fates.
> Let that goe heape a masse of wretched wealth,
>   Purchas'd by rapine, worse then stealth,
> And brooding o're it sit, with broadest eyes,
>   Not doing good, scarce when he dyes.
> Let thousands more goe flatter vice, and winne,
>   By being organes to great sinne,
> Get place, and honor, and be glad to keepe
>   The secrets, that shall breake their sleepe:
> And, so they ride in purple, eate in plate,
>   Though poyson, thinke it a great fate.

174

In opposition to such deviations Jonson invokes an ideal of attitude and behaviour that is both humanist and Christian. Clearly he is not 'a religious poet,' like Herbert or Hopkins, and of the specifically devotional poems perhaps only the sombrely powerful 'To Heaven' would demand inclusion in a short selection from his non-dramatic work. But there is Christian feeling in, for example, 'An Elegie on the Lady Jane Paulet,' where his recurring sense of life as merely 'lent'

> – Goe now, her happy Parents, and be sad
> If you not understand, what Child you had,
> If you dare grudge at Heaven, and repent
> T'have paid againe a blessing was but lent –

joins with a vision of transience not unworthy to stand beside Prospero's:

> If you can cast about your either eye
> And see all dead here, or about to dye!
> The Starres, that are the Jewels of the Night,
> And Day, deceasing! with the Prince of light!
> The Sunne! great Kings! and mightiest Kingdomes fall!
> Whole Nations! nay, Mankind! the World, with all
> That ever had beginning there, to 'ave end!
> With what injustice should one soul pretend
> T'escape this common knowne necessitie ...

The sense of *that* – the sense also that only Christian virtue can lift a man above the wretchedness of knowing it (ll. 95–100) lies behind all Jonson's poems about man as a social being and implicitly places the worldly scene he writes about, as in the superb passage in *The Staple of News* (III.ii):

> What need hath nature
> Of silver dishes, or gold chamber-pots?
> ... poor, and wise, she requires
> Meat only; hunger is not ambitious ...

175

In the poems the sobering recognition of natural limits is not too much insisted on; it simply provides a background and a tone.

Often in Jonson it is the tone that largely determines the meaning. In a world not always amenable to our desires a man must be firmly centred in himself. But Jonson's way of putting this not very recondite truth is completely free from the touch of braggadocio that one finds in Chapman's Senecal heroes.

> *He that is round within himselfe, and streight,*
> *Need seek no other strength, no other height ...*
> *Be always to thy gather'd selfe the same ...*

Thus to Sir Thomas Roe; and to Selden –

> *you that have beene*
> *Ever at home: yet, have all Countries scene:*
> *And like a Compass keeping one foot still*
> *Upon your Center, doe your Circle fill*
> *Of general knowledge ...*

To another recipient ('An Epistle to Master Arth: Squib') he writes,

> *looke, if he be*
> *Friend to himselfe, that would be friend to thee.*
> *For that is first requir'd, A man be his owne, –*

though he adds, characteristically,

> *But he that's too much that, is friend of none.*

The same note is struck in the beautiful close of 'To the World,' where Jonson clearly speaks through the persona of the 'gentle-woman, vertuous and noble' for whom it was written:

> *No, I doe know, that I was borne*
> *To age, misfortune, sicknesse, griefe:*

176

> *But I will beare these, with that scorne,*
>   *As shall not need thy false reliefe.*
> *Nor for my peace will I goe farre,*
>   *As wandrers doe, that still doe rome,*
> *But make my strengths, such as they are,*
>   *Here in my bosome, and at home.*

And, for a last example, in 'An Epistle answering to one that asked to be Sealed of the Tribe of Ben:'

> *Live to that point I will, for which I am man,*
> *And dwell as in my Center, as I can,*
> *Still looking too, and ever loving heaven;*
> *With reverence using all the gifts thence given.*
> *'Mongst which, if I have any friendships sent*
> *Such as are square, wel-tagde, and permanent,*
> *Not built with Canvasse, paper, and false lights*
> *As are the glorious scenes, at the great sights ...*
> *But all so cleare, and led by reasons flame,*
> *As but to stumble in her sight were shame,*
> *These I will honour, love, embrace, and serve.*

With 'square' (stoutly and strongly built) and 'wel-tagde' (the parts firmly joined) a further aspect of the cluster of qualities that Jonson most valued comes into view. The good life does not simply grow ('like a tree,' as he puts it in the Cary-Morison Ode); it is something made, the parts properly ordered. Vincent Corbet's was

> *A life that knew nor noise, nor strife:*
> *But was by sweetning so his will,*
> *All order, and Disposure, still.*

In this touching poem Corbet's life is compared to his well-kept gardens. In the Cary-Morison Ode the well-lived life, however short, is compared to a well-made poem —

> *for life doth her great actions spell,*
> *By what was done and wrought*
> *In season, and so brought*
> *To light: her measures are, how well*
> *Each syllab'e answer'd, and was form'd, how faire;*
> *These make the lines of life, and that's her ayre.*[14]

To *make* something, moreover, is to act:

> *Yet we must more then move still, or goe on,*
> *We must accomplish,*
>> ['An Epistle to Sir Edward Sacvile']

and in the world of necessary action the poet has his right-
ful place. It is his awareness that the poet has a recognized
social role

> *— Although to write be lesser than to doo,*
>> *It is the next deed, and a great one too —*
>> ['To Sir Henry Savile']

that allows Jonson his tone of manly independence.
We all know that he told Drummond, 'he never esteemed
of a man for the name of a lord' — 'the cork of title' that
keeps some men afloat — a claim that is borne out not only
by explicit declarations in the poems

> *— That some word*
> *Might be found out as good, and not* my Lord.
> *That Nature no such difference had imprest*
> *In men, but every bravest was the best:*
> *That blood not mindes, but mindes did blood adorne —*
>> ['To Sir William Jephson']

but above all by the tone of such things as the 'Epistle to
Sir Edward Sacvile, Now Earle of Dorset' (*The Under-
wood*, XIII). Perhaps we may recall here the splendid col-
location (and the order of reference to the two monarchs)

when he praises Lord Lisle's hospitality in the famous address 'To Penshurst' :

> *... all is there;*
> *As if thou, then, wert mine, or I reign'd here:*
> *There's nothing I can wish, for which I stay.*
> *That found King James, when hunting late, this way ...*

It will be obvious from these references and quotations (and not unfamiliar to any reader of the poems) that the values Jonson most prized have a social reference. And most of his poems – there are exceptions – are directly or indirectly concerned with the expression of those values. The poems therefore are not simply a miscellaneous collection; they form a coherent body of work, unified by certain major themes. These have been so well described by Hugh Maclean that all I need do here by way of summary is to borrow from his excellent essay.[15] In the poems, he says, 'we find ... not an explicit and detailed outline of the social order Jonson admired, but rather "notes" on particular elements that ought to mark a society properly ordered, as well as suggestions for conduct in the midst of a disordered one. The negative strictures of the comedies, accordingly, are supplemented and completed by positive advice in the poetry and *Discoveries.*' The three main themes are 'the virtue of friendship between good men, who are receptive by nature to the free exchange of opinion and counsel, and the strong resource such friendships constitute for the ordered society and the secure state'; the relations that ideally should obtain between prince – or aristocratic patron – and poet; and 'the social attitudes and actions befitting a "ruling class" which thoroughly understands the nature of its responsibilities and desires to make them effective.' Even in his panegyrics, of course, Jonson does not offer a map of 'upper-class' society in his day, only a map of what it might be and ought to be. He was, incidentally, a master of the device of advising by praising.[16] Perhaps all that needs to be added to Maclean's account is some recognition of the *extension* of Jonson's feeling for the necessary interrelationships between men of different parts and functions to include the dependence of all on a given 'Nature,' as in 'To Penshurst.'[17] The less well known Epithalamion for the marriage of Hierome Weston and Lady Frances Stuart embodies in its ingeniously woven verse an even more widely embracing sense of relationship – of days and seasons, of the generations, of court and country, king and subjects, man and nature.

It remains to ask why poems so firmly attached to a particular time and place should still be read today for other than historical reasons. A short answer is that Jonson does more than describe public or quasi-public qualities that are valuable in any social order, he does so *as a poet*: that is, there is an inherent perennial vitality in the poems that, as in all good poetry, calls out a corresponding energy of apprehension in the responsive reader. What this means in turn is that we are concerned with a particular *style*, which not only conveys the particular subject matter, but in its own individual way goes beyond the paraphrasable sense, beyond whatever it was that Jonson first wrote as a prose draft.

In our understanding of the poetry we all owe a particular debt to Wesley Trimpi, whose study of 'the plain style' has done so much to help us get the perspective right. What I have now to say can be regarded as a supplementary note to Trimpi's work, with – since I lack his classical learning – rather different emphases from his own. Whatever Jonson owed to the classical – or, to a lesser extent – the native plain style,[18] the individual accent, as Trimpi of course admits, is what makes any study of context or tradition worth while. In defining the peculiarly Jonsonian manner we do well to call to mind the combined delicacy and firmness in the verse movement of the songs in the masques and plays. In the more intimate of the poems – the epitaphs on his first daughter, on his first son, and on Salomon Pavy (*Epigrammes*, XXII, XLV, CXX) – the studied lack of insistence makes the subtle rhythmic variations the more effective, as in the almost undefinably moving,

> *This grave partakes the fleshly birth.*
> *Which cover lightly, gentle earth.*

In another epitaph, on Vincent Corbet, 'classical' simplicity and restraint are similarly married to the tones and rhythms of personal feeling.

> *No stubbornnesse so stiffe, nor folly*
> *To licence ever was so light,*
> *As twice to trespasse in his sight,*
> *His lookes would so correct it, when*
> *It chid the vice, yet not the Men.*
> *Much from him I professe I wonne,*
> *And more, and more, I should have done,*
> *But that I understood him scant;*
> *Now I conceive him by my want ...*

The plain style, then, is not neutral or colourless.[19] Jonson's verse (which demands to be read aloud, with a feeling for 'the *sound* of sense') has not the obvious richness of texture of Donne's, but it has its own quasi-dramatic way of rendering movements of mind and feeling.

> *Though you sometimes proclaim me too severe,*
> *Rigid, and harsh, which is a Drug austere*
> *In friendship, I confesse: But deare friend, heare.*
> ['An Epistle to a Friend,' *The Under-wood*, XXXVII]

Or, addressing Selden,

> *Which Grace shall I make love too first? your skill*
> *Or faith in things? or is't your wealth and will*
> *T'instruct and teach? or your unweary'd paine*
> *Of Gathering, Bountie in pouring out againe?*
> > [*The Under-wood*, xiv]

— where in the last line quoted the syllables crowded into the rhythmic unit before the unexpectedly early caesura suggest something of Selden's close-packed labours, and the second part of the line, from the reversed stress of 'Bountie,' seems to pour itself out with something of Selden's own abundance.

It is because Jonson's verse possesses resources such as these that the poems still capture the imagination when they speak to friends and patrons of different aspects of a shared social world. The epigram addressed to Sir Henry Nevil (*Epigrammes*, cix) both sums up Jonson's ideal for a man with a part to play in his country's affairs and the poet's relation to such men, and finely exhibits the qualities that I have tried to indicate.

> *Who now calls on thee, Nevil, is a Muse,*
> *That serves nor fame, nor titles; but doth chuse*
> *Where vertue makes them both, and that's in thee:*
> *Where all is faire, beside thy pedigree.*
> *Thou are not one, seek'st miseries with hope,*
> *Wrestlest with dignities, or fain'st a scope*
> *Of service to the publique, when the end*
> *Is private gaine, which hath long guilt to friend.*
> *Thou rather striv'st the matter to possesse,*
> *And elements of honour, then the dresse;*
> *To make thy lent life, good against the Fates:*
> *And first to know thine owne state, then the States.*
> *To be the same in roote, thou art in height;*
> *And that thy soule should give thy flesh her weight.*
> *Goe on, and doubt not, what posteritie,*
> *Now I have sung thee thus, shall judge of thee.*

> *Thy deedes, unto thy name, will prove new wombes,*
> *Whil'st others toyle for titles to their tombes.*

In the first eight lines the defining is mainly by negatives ('a Muse, That serves nor fame, nor titles,' 'Thou art not one...'). As the poem moves to the celebration of Nevil's qualities the verse texture thickens and engages the reader more closely.

> *Thou rather striv'st the matter to possesse,*
> *And elements of honor, then the dresse;*
> *To make thy lént life, good against the Fates:*
> *And first to know thine oẃne státe, thén the States.*
> *To be the same in roote, thou art in height;*
> *And that thy soúle should give thy flésh hér weíght.*
> *Góe ón ...*

The changing pattern of stresses, the cluster of emphases, the reinforcement of allied consonants and vowels – all help to give the sense of steady movement, of actively engaging with life, ending with the finely dismissive,

> *Whil'st others tóyle for títles to their tombes.*

Jonson's verse, I have tried to indicate, is indeed 'plain,' as Trimpi defines it, but not in any limiting sense. It has its music: something that suggests that, for all the hard rationality of his mind, it had its origins, at its best, not far from those regions where very different poets have first sensed their meanings in 'a wordless musical stir.' I should like to end by quoting 'To the Right Honourable, the Lord High Treasurer of England. An Epistle Mendicant. 1631' (*The Under-wood*, LXXI), even though Trimpi has already called attention to its moving qualities. The poem is not public in the sense of dealing directly with the behaviour and attitudes of public men, but it does reflect Jonson's convictions about the role of the poet in a world of men concerned with public affairs.

My Lord;
Poore wretched states, prest by extremities,
Are faine to seeke for succours, and supplies
Of Princes aides, or good mens Charities.

Disease, the Enemie, and his Ingineeres,
Wants, with the rest of his conceal'd compeeres,
Have cast a trench about mee, now five yeares.

And made those strong approaches, by False braies,
Reduicts, Halfe-moones, Horne-workes, and such
    close wayes,
The Muse not peepes out, one of hundred dayes;

But lyes block'd up, and straightned, narrow'd in,
Fix'd to the bed, and boords, unlike to win
Health, or scarce breath, as she had never bin.

Unless some saving-Honour of the Crowne,
Dare thinke it, to relieve, no lesse renowne,
A Bed-rid Wit, then a besieged Towne.

The poem, although explicitly a begging letter, is 'manly, and not smelling parasite,' confessing the poet's wants and sufferings (it was written five years after his paralytic stroke[20]), but dissolving self-pity in a witty metaphor. Compact and firm, it reflects the kind of life that Jonson most admired – 'All order, and Disposure still.'[21] But the order is not imposed or inert; as an expression of a genuinely 'resolved soul,' it has an unmistakable vitality.

It is, I suppose, vitality – a life-enhancing energy – that is common to all good poetry, of whatever kind. In reading any dozen or so of Jonson's 'social' poems at a stretch we do indeed feel that we are in contact with the mind of a man who stands for social-moral attitudes, for shared, traditional norms, that it would be damaging to allow to be edged away to the fringes of our collective consciousness just because they are not so exciting as many other things that claim our attention in literature. But it is an individual, powerful, and distinctive mind – with its own privacies. That is why poems that spring from and reflect a particular social milieu live on, independent of it.

NOTES

1 Incidentally, even here it is impossible to define exact boundaries: *The Waste Land* is a depiction of certain recurring aspects of men's life together that are parallel to, or expressive of, the poet's personal and private existence.

2 J.B. Bamborough, *Ben Jonson*, Hutchinson's University Library (London 1970), 159–60

3 The obvious and inescapable reference here is to Lawrence Stone, *The Crisis of the Aristocracy, 1558–1641* (Oxford 1965) especially ch. 5, section 2 ('The Face of Violence') and ch. 3 ('Office and the Court').

4 '... if I have praysed, unfortunately, any one, that doth not deserve, or, if all answere not, in all numbers, the pictures I have made of them: I hope it will be forgiven me, that they be no ill pieces, though they be not like the persons.' *Epigrammes*, Dedication (Muses' Library Edition of Jonson's *Poems*, ed. George Burke Johnston [Cambridge, Mass. 1954] 5. I have used this edition throughout.)

5 See Stone, *Crisis of the Aristocracy*, ch. 12 ('Education and Culture'), especially section 5 (i) ('Literature and Scholarship'), and Patricia Thomson, 'The Literature of Patronage, 1580–1630,' *Essays in Criticism*, II (1952).

6 *Ben Jonson and the Language of Prose Comedy* (Cambridge, Mass. 1960), 279

7 Ted Hughes, *Poetry in the Making* (London 1967), 17

8 *Conversations with Drummond*, in *Ben Jonson*, ed. C.H. Herford and P. and E. Simpson, 11 vols (Oxford 1925–52), I, 143

9 Jacques Maritain, *Creative Intuition in Art and Poetry*, ch. 8 ('The Internalization of Music'). Nadezhda Mandel-

stam, *Hope against Hope* (tr. Max Hayward, London 1971), 70, 187

10 For a striking example, see Jon Stallworthy's account of the making of 'The Second Coming,' *Agenda* (autumn-winter 1971–2), 24–33. Stallworthy refers to his *Between the Lines: Yeats's Poetry in the Making* (Oxford 1963) which I have not read.

11 T.S. Eliot, preface to Leone Vivante, *English Poetry and its Contribution to the Knowledge of a Creative Principle* (Urbana, IL 1963), ix–x

12 Wesley Trimpi, *Ben Jonson's Poems: A Study of the Plain Style* (Stanford, Cal. 1962), 105ff

13 For 'Poetry as Discovery' I may refer to my essay in *Reality and Creative Vision in German Lyrical Poetry*, ed. A. Closs (London 1964). For 'The Hinterland of Thought' see D.W. Harding's essay with that title in his *Experience into Words* (London 1963).

14 The analogy has of course been used by other poets, notably Eliot. To be 'free' (which, as Hugh Maclean notices, is a recurring word in the poems) is to accept order and discipline. In a poem to the Countess of Bedford (*Epigrammes*, LXXVI) Jonson writes of his ideal woman:

> *Onely a learned, and a manly soule*
> *I purpos'd her; that should, with even powers,*
> *The rock* [distaff], *the spindle, and the sheeres*
>   *controule*
> *Of destinie, and spin her own free houres.*

Naturally Jonson knew that no one could control the shears of Atropos. A man or woman is only 'free' in the sense that, within recognized and accepted limits, he acts in accordance with his own integrity, and does not leave his proper sphere of action 'to wracke on a strange shelf.' (This memorable image is from the poem, 'To Sir Robert Wroth': 'God wisheth, none should wracke on a strange shelf; / To him, man's dearer, then t'himselfe.' *The Forrest*, III.)

15 Hugh Maclean, 'Ben Jonson's Poems: Notes on an Ordered Society,' in *Essays in English Literature from the Renaissance to the Victorian Age, Presented to A.S.P. Wood-*

house, ed. M. MacLure and F.W. Watt (Toronto 1964).
See also Geoffrey Walton, *From Metaphysical to Augustan: Studies in Tone and Sensibility in the Seventeenth Century* (London 1955), ch. 2, 'The Tone of Ben Jonson's Poetry.'

16 See the admission in 'An Epistle to Master John Selden' (*The Under-wood,* XIV):

> *Though I confesse (as every Muse hath err'd,*
> *And mine not least) I have too oft preferr'd*
> *Men, past their termes, and prais'd some names too*
> *   much,*
> *But 'twas with purpose to have made them such.*

17 For the grounding of this poem in actuality see J.C.A. Rathmell, 'Jonson, Lord Lisle, and Penshurst,' *English Literary Renaissance,* I, 3 (Autumn 1971); also G.R. Hibbard, 'The Country House Poem of the Seventeenth Century,' *Journal of the Warburg and Courtauld Institute,* XIX (1956), 159ff.

18 Recognition of the virtues of the native plain style has been made easier by practitioners and critics such as Yvor Winters and J.V. Cunningham. See also the introduction to John Williams, *English Renaissance Poetry: A Collection of Shorter Poems from Skelton to Jonson* (New York 1962) with its interesting shift of emphasis from older anthologies in the choice of poems.

19 '[Jonson said] That verses stood by sense, without either colours or accent, which yet (Drummond adds) other times he denied.' *Conversations,* Herford and Simpson, I, 143

20 For Jonson's personal circumstances at this time, see Herford and Simpson, I, 91ff.

21 In defining the tone of this, it is interesting to compare the more excited movement of the couplet in *The Vanity of Human Wishes* that uses a similar metaphor (ll. 281–2, 'Unnumbered maladies his joints invade ...'), which is of course splendid in a different way.

MEMBERS OF THE
CONFERENCE

BAKER, JEFFREY St Francis Xavier University
BARISH, JONAS University of California, Berkeley
BAXTER, JOHN S. Queen's University
BEECHER, D.A. Carleton University
BELL, MICHAEL Ithaca College
BELL, SUSAN C. State University of New York, Binghamton
BENTLEY, G.E. Princeton University
BLISSETT, W.F. University College, University of Toronto
BLOSTEIN, DAVID Victoria College, University of Toronto
BOND, RONALD B. University College, University of
    Toronto
BRADY, JENNIFER Victoria College, University of Toronto
BRADY, KRISTIN University of Toronto
BURNS, DOROTHY State University of New York,
    Binghamton
BURNS, NORMAN T. State University of New York,
    Binghamton
CARSCALLEN, J. Victoria College, University of Toronto
CIORAN, SHARON University of London

COCKE, WILLIAM T., III University of the South, Tennessee
COHEN, DEREK M. York University
COLDWELL, JOAN McMaster University
COOK, ALBERT State University of New York, Buffalo
CORMAN, BRIAN Erindale College, University of Toronto
CRAWLEY, D.F. Queen's University
CRUTTWELL, PATRICK Carleton University
DAVIES, ROBERTSON Massey College, University of
   Toronto
DE GROOT, H.B. University College, University of Toronto
DE MATTEIS, DAVID University of Toronto
DE QUEHEN, A.H. University College, University of
   Toronto
DESSEN, ALAN C. Northwestern University
DORRELL, MARGARET University of Sydney
DREW-BEAR, ANNETTE Loyola of Montreal
DUBLIN, H. York University
DYSON, J.P. New College, University of Toronto
ENDICOTT, N.J. University College, University of Toronto
FALLE, GEORGE G. Trinity College, University of Toronto
FELPERIN, HOWARD University of California, Santa Barbara
FERNS, JOHN McMaster University
FISHER, ADELE University of Toronto
FOX, A.G. University of Western Ontario
FRIESEN, BRUNO Algonquin College
FRIESEN, HELGA C. Algonquin College
FRYE, NORTHROP Massey College, University of Toronto
GAINES, BARRY J. University of Tennessee
GALLOWAY, DAVID University of New Brunswick
GARDINER, JUDITH K. University of Illinois at Chicago
   Circle
GARLOCK, GAYLE N. London, Ontario
GILLING, TED University of Toronto
GLOBE, ALEXANDER University of British Columbia
GREENE, R.A. Faculty of Arts and Science, University
   of Toronto

GRICE, GERDA H. Drama Centre, University of Toronto
GRICE, DERMOT H. University of Toronto
HALPENNY, FRANCESS University of Toronto
HAMILTON, JAMES S. Queen's University
HARLEY, GRAHAM D. University College, University of
  Toronto
HEDRICK, DON Cornell University
HIBBARD, GEORGE Waterloo University
HOENIGER, DAVID Victoria College, University of Toronto
HOLMES, D.M. University of Windsor
HOSEK, CHAVIVA Victoria College, University of Toronto
HOWARD-HILL, TREVOR University of South Carolina
HUMEZ, JEAN M. Boston University
HUNTE, ESMÉ University of Toronto
HUNTER, MARTIN Drama Centre, University of Toronto
HUNTLEY, FRANK L. University of Michigan
HUSSEY, MAURICE Cambridge College of Arts and
  Technology
HYLAND, PETER McMaster University
JAMIESON, JEAN C. University of Toronto Press
JOHNSTON, ALEXANDRA F. Victoria College, University of
  Toronto
JOHNSTON, KEVIN Queen's University
JONES, ROBERT C. Ohio State University
KANE, SEAN Scarborough College, University of Toronto
KAPLAN, JOEL H. University of British Columbia
KAPLAN, SALLY B. State University of New York,
  Binghamton
KAREDA, URJO Erindale College, University of Toronto
KAY, W. DAVID University of Illinois
KESLER, R. LINCOLN University of Toronto
KIRKLEY, N.H. University of British Columbia
KNIGHTS, L.C. Queen's College, Cambridge
KUHN, JOAQUIN St Michael's College, University of
  Toronto
KUIN, ROGER York University

LAING, MICHAEL University of Toronto

LANCASHIRE, A. University College, University of Toronto

LANCASHIRE, IAN Erindale College, University of Toronto

LAWRY, J.S. Laurentian University

LEBANS, WILLIAM University College, University of Toronto

LEECH, CLIFFORD University College, University of Toronto

LEGGATT, A.M. University College, University of Toronto

LE PAN, DOUGLAS University of Toronto

LEVENSON, J. Trinity College, University of Toronto

LEVIN, RICHARD State University of New York, Stony Brook

LINDHEIM, NANCY Trinity College, University of Toronto

LISTER, R. University of Waterloo

LOEFFLER, WILLIAM R. State University of New York, Stony Brook

LOEFFLER, SHERYL E. State University of New York, Stony Brook

MACCALLUM, H.R. University College, University of Toronto

MCKENZIE, D.F. Victoria University of Wellington

MACLEAN, HUGH State University of New York, Albany

MCLUHAN, MARSHALL Centre for Culture and Technology, University of Toronto

MADER, LEONARD University of Western Ontario

MARCHALONIS, SHIRLEY L. Slippery Rock State College

MARGESON, J.M.R. Scarborough College, University of Toronto

MARINELLI, PETER V. University College, University of Toronto

MAROTTI, ARTHUR F. Wayne State University

MATSON, MARSHALL University of Guelph

MILLGATE, MICHAEL University College, University of Toronto

MILLS, LLOYD L. Kent State University

MUIRHEAD, JOHN Massey College, University of Toronto
NATHAN, DEBBY University of Toronto
NEILL, MARY University of Western Ontario
NEUFELD, EVELYN State University of New York, Fredonia
NORLAND, HOWARD B. University of Nebraska
OVERALL, FRANCIS Greenville, Tennessee
OWEN, PATRICIA City University of New York
PATRICK, JULIAN Victoria College, University of Toronto
PEK, SISTER ANNELLA University of Toronto
PRATT, DONALD S. University of Western Ontario
PRITCHARD, ALLAN University College, University of
    Toronto
RAMSEY, JOHN S. State University of New York, Fredonia
RASPA, ANTHONY Dalhousie University
REED, R. State University of New York, Fredonia
REIBETANZ, JOHN Victoria College, University of Toronto
RETTER, CRAIG University of Toronto
SADDLEMYER, ANN Drama Centre, University of Toronto
SALERNO, HENRY F. State University of New York,
    Fredonia
SALTER, DENIS Drama Centre, University of Toronto
SALVATORE, BRUCE St Francis Xavier University
SHAND, G.B. Glendon College, York University
SHAPIRO, MICHAEL University of Illinois
SHEN, JANE University of Toronto
SMITH, D.I.B. University College, University of Toronto
STEDMOND, J.M. Queen's University
SYLVESTER, WILLIAM State University of New York,
    Buffalo
TAIT, MICHAEL S. Scarborough College, University of
    Toronto
TAYLOR, JAMES O. St Francis Xavier University
TAYLOR, MICHAEL J.H. University of New Brunswick
THOMAS, MARY OLIVE Georgia State University
THOMPSON, SISTER GERALDINE St Michael's College,
    University of Toronto

This book

was designed by

ROBERT MACDONALD

under the direction of

ALLAN FLEMING